"Isaias Powers has done it again! He has skillfully woven together a collection of elements that result in a truly inspirational prayerbook — a book *of prayer,* a book *for prayer.* Powers demonstrates in this work an amazing ability to introduce us into the mystery of the Incarnation in a manner that reverences the divinity and enhances the humanity of Jesus Christ, through the eyes of his mother, Mary.

"The first part of every chapter is instructive, drawing on information gleaned from the author's own reading, study and reflection. The latter part is an invitation to prayer through an appeal to the reader's imagination and *dynamic memory.* He engages us totally, linking our experience with those of the mother of God in simple, yet practical ways. . . This is a book for those who wish to grow in prayer and in a deeper knowledge and love of Mary of Nazareth."

Sr. Agnes Cunningham, SSCM
St. Mary of the Lake Seminary
Mundelein, Illinois

"Father Powers provides Gospel words and settings to our daily problems, frustrations and hopes. It is consoling to realize quietly that Mary faced the same round of questions. It is strengthening when our questions turn into quiet moments of prayer in the presence of Jesus. Here gospel study and kindly human experience are put to our service. I hope and pray this book will reach many homes and into the hearts of people where it will do much good."

Rev. Carroll Stuhlmueller, CP
Catholic Theological Union
Chicago, Illinois

"Father Powers writes along the lines of a respected tradition. Christian authors from early days have reflected prayerfully on the intervals in the lives of Jesus and Mary his Mother, intervals the Gospels pass over in silence. Fr. Powers has pondered the Gospels and read between the lines, looking into the hidden lives of Jesus and Mary for events reflected in the Savior's stories and parables.

"In their joint pastoral, *Behold Your Mother, Woman of Faith,* the bishops of the United States said, 'There were also joyous years at Nazareth, as her Son grew to adulthood, and something of the happiness of the Holy Family comes through in the gospel preaching of Jesus with his tender examples from home life.'

"Father Powers offers 'God's upbeat messages,' for example...on the coin which was lost, and was found...on Cana...on Mary after Cana....on Jesus' own quiet years with Mary and Joseph.

"The first half of the book covers the childhood of Jesus, then his teens and twenties; the second takes up the public life into the passion and resurrection, and with rich imagination 'Mary, with her new family, after Easter.' Each chapter begins with a Gospel quotation, and concludes with a prayer, applying the reflection to the reader in a very personal way."

Rev. Eamon R. Carroll, O. Carm.
Professor of Theology
Loyola University of Chicago

Dear Cathy

Rev. Isaias Powers, C.P.
Author of Quiet Places with Jesus

something different in each book.

Quiet Places with Mary

love, Isaias

37 "Guided Imagery" Meditations

a ka of the

TWENTY-THIRD PUBLICATIONS
Mystic, Connecticut

Seventh printing 1998

Twenty-Third Publications
185 Willow Street
P.O. Box 180
Mystic, CT 06355
(860) 536-2611
800-321-0411

ISBN 0-89622-297-7
Library of Congress Catalog Card Number 86-50123
Printed in U.S.A.

The cover photo: Madonna and Child sculpture is located in the Passionist House of Greater Solitude in Bedford, Pennsylvania.

Contents

Part Three: Mary, With Jesus During His Active Ministry

Part Four: Mary, With Her New Family, After Easter

Forethoughts

A few years ago, I wrote *Quiet Places with Jesus.* It has been very popular. It seems to fit a need. This book is a sister piece to the other. It too may provide a service for busy people who find it difficult to "switch gears" after a hectic day and settle down enough so that prayer may happen.

The method is the same. A text is selected, with just those gospel phrases that fit the reflection. Commentary is provided so that the readers can see connections between Jesus and Mary and themselves. Guided imagery is suggested to provide the memory and imagination with a fixed location of time, space, and situation so that other distractions may be suppressed. Once this happens, the person in prayer can become more hopeful that God may want to use this quiet time to enter the soul with either a sense of his presence or some practical inspirations in the areas of change of heart, courage in afflictions, service to others, or consolations for self.

The book is divided into four parts:

Part One: Mary, When Jesus Was a Child
Part Two: Mary, When Jesus Was in His Teens and Twenties
Part Three: Mary, With Jesus During His Public Life
Part Four: Mary, With Her New Family, After Easter

The first and third parts follow the actual data of the gospels. The second part is pure guesswork. Texts are taken from the time of Christ's active ministry. These gospel passages are considered as "clues" attesting to the way Jesus grew up during his hidden years. They are nothing more than conjecture on my part. I have received no direct visions by which I make absolute claim to their credibility, but they do have a kind of intuitive truthfulness. Jesus "grew in wisdom and favor" by learning from his parents and from the everyday occupations that filled out his life. I simply guessed about what some of those particulars might have been, based on the record we have of him.

The fourth part is different also. When I prayed over Mary's influence on the early church, there was only one clue to guide me. Mary was present with the disciples at Pentecost. How was her presence felt? We don't know. But we can presume it was a powerful influence for good. I let the sense of this influence be expressed indirectly: through the lips of different narrators telling the story of those times.

"Telling the story" is the basis of all these chapters. They are not data for research. They are meant to help prayer, not to provide additional revelation on the life of Christ.

In a very important way, they are true to the gospel message. Jesus chose to teach by means of stories. The parables of our Lord were not intended to provide all the answers, nor end all further thought. They were told in order to elicit curiosity, augment further pondering, provide a frame for personal prayer.

Christ's stories were "teasers of truth" told so that his audiences would want to learn more. They were invitations to further education about the nature of God and the human responses necessary for taking part in his kingdom.

Mark's gospel understands Christ's teaching method this way: "When Jesus was alone, the disciples asked him about the parables. And he said to them, 'To you it is given to know the mystery of the kingdom of God; but to those (who do not inquire further) all things are treated in parables'" (4:10-11). "In many parables, Jesus spoke the word to them, according as they were able to understand. Without a parable he did not speak to them. But privately he explained all things to his disciples" (4:33-34).

The four dots that honeycomb each guided imagery prayer are recommendations for silence. They urge the reader to put down the book and ask what the disciples asked in Mark, to learn more, privately, about the stories told by Jesus . . . and about the stories suggested in this book.

Both Mary and Jesus are the main storytellers in these chapters. One does not speak without the presence of the other. They are a team. Still, Mary is much more "on stage" than she is in the gospels. What are the grounds for giving her such pre-eminence? How do I see her role as the "spiritual guide for personal prayer?" I call on two authors to help me explain the direction of this book. Coventry Patmore said, "Mary is our one salvation from an abstract Christ."

Mary is not our salvation. Jesus is. He alone. But Mary saves us from turning her son into an abstract function for our own designs. Many people make Jesus an abstraction. They first have a bone to pick or a cause to champion. They then "fit Christ's words" into their scheme. It is a kind of manipulation, using parts of the gospel to further their own ends.

Mary prevents this kind of warping. Thanks to her, we remember that Jesus had his flesh and blood. Jesus was a human part of a human family. He lived in a specific village and was nurtured by normal growth. These incarnate facts force us to let Jesus speak for himself in all his complexity. With Mary to remind us about the humanity of the Word of God, Jesus stands as the paramount figure in prayer. We learn that we must fit into his message and his method of presenting his message. We do not abstract Jesus by making our ideas paramount and forcing his message to fit our ideas.

The other author is Frank Baum, writer of *The Wizard of Oz*. I see Glenda, the Good Witch of the North, as a Mary figure. She was a background personage; the Wizard was in the foreground. She simply did two things: She showed Dorothy that she cared about her (giving her assurance and suggesting she wear the red shoes); also, she guided Dorothy to the yellow brick road, recommending her to the Wizard. The Wizard would be the one who would help her.

That is Mary's role. At Cana she tells her son, "They have no wine." (That is: "I care about the bride and groom and their families. I want you to help them, son.") Then Mary said to the attendants: "Do whatever he tells you." (That is: "I want you to follow my son's instructions.")

Mary continues through history in her Cana role. She is our mother who loves us with maternal care, and she is our guide to Jesus. She leads us on the right path so that we may be helped by Christ . . . and be ready to "do whatever he tells us."

This, then, is a book of stories—stories that may help your quiet prayer. They are of value only in so far as they open possibilities for Jesus to inspire you with his private explanations, his own way of teaching you further about his kingdom. Words and images are good only if they lead to the silence of "sensed presence with God."

I will conclude in the same way I did in *Quiet Places With Jesus*:

> "May Mary, the greatest example of prayer, guide you to a place of peace . . . and to such a habit of constant prayer that you will no longer need manuals or methods . . . when God will speak plainly— without parables—to your heart."

PART ONE

Mary

When Jesus Was a Child

1

Freed From Blame

When the angel had come, he said to her, "Do not be afraid, Mary; for you have found favor with God. You shall conceive and shall bring forth a son and you shall call his name Jesus. . . . "The Holy Spirit shall come upon you and the Power of the Most High shall overshadow you. . . . " And Mary said, "Behold the maidservant of the Lord. Let it be done to me according to (his) word."

Luke 1:28-38

Reflection

Mary's prayer is different from the style of prayer described by the Baltimore Catechism. The Catechism definition is: "A lifting up of the heart and mind to God." Mary's method is a "letting be—a letting it be done, as God wills."

"Lifting up" implies energy expended on our part. It suggests human initiative, calling for God's response. ("Okay, God, I'm lifting up my heart and mind. Now do something!")

4

Mary's way is much more subdued, much less forward. "Lifting up" is active. "Letting be" is passive. There is a world of difference in the two.

Prayer is better explained by Mary's descriptive definition. She didn't do anything. The initiative was God's. This does not mean that prayer happens without effort. There is effort. But the effort is preliminary to the prayer itself. That is how it was with Mary. The Holy Spirit did the actual work. She simply made herself available for the work of love to happen.

The first three mediations of this book consider the triple "letting go-letting be" exercises that Mary had to undertake before she could be in the position to let it be done to her by God. Like every human, she had to clear away all the obstacles that would have prevented her from being open to God's possibilities.

First, and most essential, Mary had to let go of the past—all the hurts of her life, all the grudges people had against her. She had to leave the memory of those bad feelings behind her.

Can anyone realistically imagine that Mary was never hurt by certain individuals in her life? Has anyone, ever, been freed from such experiences? Just because we don't know who they were does not mean there weren't obnoxious and malicious people in her life. Maybe it was a member of her family who wouldn't speak to her. Maybe it was a group of girls her own age who were jealous and mean. Maybe a spiteful neighbor was making life difficult for her. Maybe . . . even probably. . . .

If Mary had not let go of these hurts, she would not have been present for God's Annunciation. Using the analogy of a telephone call, the angel's message would not have "gotten through," because the lines would have been "busy" with her preoccupations. The mind would have been cluttered by all the people in her life whom she could blame for having done her harm.

The point is not that Mary had a right to be hurt. Everyone has a right to be hurt, for everyone has been treated unfairly by somebody. The point is freedom, not justice. Justice keeps insisting, "I have a right to be righteously indignant!" But freedom refuses to claim this right. It answers to a higher responsibility: "I have a duty to disengage myself from the memory of those who have hurt me in the past. If I don't free myself from those hurts, I cannot be open to the possibilities of the present time!"

Obviously, Mary was not locked in to the memory of experiences that could have agitated or distressed her. She couldn't change the past. It would be a useless waste of energy to keep returning to situations where friends or family behaved in unloving ways toward her. These remembered scenes would only cause flare-ups in her heart. She let go. Consequently, she was able to let be.

Mary will help us learn to understand this most essential beginning of prayer. Unless we let go of our hurts, we will never be open to anything but our right to be upset. Mary will soften our grip on our grudges. She will be gentle—and forceful—about freeing us from the deadliest obstacle of all: the tendency to blame ourselves, and others, for the wrongs that have happened in the past.

In dealing with all our yesterdays, we must say, "Let it go!" Then we will be able to respond as graciously as Mary; and we will be able to say to his messages of grace: "Let it be . . . as the Lord would have it be."

Prayer

In your imagination, think of a deep pool,
fed by a fresh stream . . .

You are some distance away from the pool.
It is an uphill climb to get there. . . .
It is made more difficult
      because you carry two heavy rocks
      in your coat pockets. . . .

Let the heaviest rock represent the one person
      who has hurt you most deeply
      (the hurt that is hardest to forget . . .).
Let the other rock represent all the ways
      that other people have treated you unfairly. . . .

Feel uncomfortable
from the burden of carrying this heaviness. . . .

Walk slowly, painfully, uphill
until you get to the bridge crossing the pool. . . .
Meet Mary beside the bridge.
Feel her presence. . . .

Take time to be aware of her gentle compassion,
        her kindly care. . . .
In whatever way she wants to tell you,
        let her convince you
        to drop those rocks into the deepest part of the pool. . . .

(Struggle with this decision for some time.
        It would be good to be freed of the weights.
        But you have become so accustomed to living
        with righteous indignation about them,
        it is difficult to let go. . . .)

Feel Mary's presence behind you. . . .
She puts her hands on your shoulders;
        you relax at last. . . .

Finally, do as Mary says.
Let them go. . . .
Watch them as they drop out of sight. . . .
Notice how the rocks muddy the water for a while. . . .
But soon the stream washes all the dirt away
        and the rocks stay down,
        joining others in the bottom of the pool. . . .

Now you are free.
You are present to God,
available for his inspirations.
Remain present, this way, for as long as it seems good. . . .

2

Freed From Bitterness

When the angel had come [to Mary] he said to her: "Rejoice, most highly-favored daughter; the Lord is with you." When she heard him, she was troubled at his words and kept pondering what manner of greeting this might be. And the angel said to her: "Do not be afraid, Mary, for you have found favor with God. . . ." And Mary said, "Let it be done to me. . . ."

Luke 1:28-38

Reflection

God's greeting caused Mary some trouble. The messenger told her three things, all of them quite problematic for most humans. Even Mary had to ponder them over for a while.

The three ponderables did not have to do with being the mother of the divine child. That part of the message had not come yet. Before she was asked to agree to an action, she was told to agree with some statements that God was making about her. She was told to be joyful. She was told to accept the fact that God loved her (indeed, that she was highly favored!). She was told, also, to trust in God's abiding presence—the Lord was with her.

These statements present a challenge no human can easily be comfortable with. Many find them intolerable. The mood of bitterness can make it very difficult to hear such an astounding message. Bitterness is an obstacle like blame. But blame has to do with the past; bitterness is caused by the clamor and discomforts messing up the present time.

How can one respond to the call to be joyful, if the mind is chained to a sense of sadness? How can one know God's love, if the heart is weighed down by loneliness or non-love? How can one trust God's care, if the soul is consumed by discouragement, cynicism or a distrust in everything and everybody?

To some degree, we all have reasons for resonating to arguments persuading us to be bitter about our present state in life. To the degree that we listen to these messages, we won't be able to hear the bugle of God's "reveille" inviting us to begin a life of grace as Mary experienced it: "Rejoice!" "Know my love for you!" "Trust that I am with you!"

If Mary was caught in the web of discontent, she could have argued with God's messenger. She could have blocked the message and said: "How can I rejoice? Did you see how Miriam, and Naomi, and Ruth all snubbed me at the well this morning?" She could have said: "If God thinks so highly of me, why am I so poor? And why do I have this cold that I cannot get rid of?" She could have said: "If the Lord is with me, why did he let my mother and father die when I prayed and prayed that they wouldn't die?"

These are just a few things that Mary could have said—with as much justification as many others who quit on God. But she didn't resist the call to "rejoice; be loved; learn trust!" by insisting on her right to fidget or fuss over depressing situations. She "let it be." She let go of all tendencies to resent those things in life that made her uncomfortable . . . and all those things that gradually would have made her feel unlovable and unsure of trusting anyone.

She is our model in both senses of "Let it be" and "Let it go." She will help us free ourselves from the hold that discontentments have on us. We need not be trapped by bitterness, or by anybody's lack of love, or by individuals who have betrayed our trust. We are much more than the whole list of things causing us discouragements.

Let Mary prove this to be so. Let her persuade us to let go of our hold on unhappiness—so that we may be responsive when God calls us to rejoice (his way); and be loved (by him); and learn trust, once more, in his abiding presence.

Prayer

In your imagination,
take yourself to a haymeadow, surrounded by high hills.

It is a hot day in June and the bugs are fierce. . . .
No matter how much you shoo them, they will not go away.
They bother you by their nervous noise,
        and by their stings. . . .

Let these pests represent all the uncomfortable thoughts
you have about your present life:
        – things you would like, but have to do without
        – physical ailments
        – people you envy for any reason
        – missed opportunities
        – the put-downs others give you (and you give yourself)
        – the way some people don't like you, or won't accept you
        – disappointments over unanswered prayer
        – the loss of a loved-one. . . .

Feel this situation—all these bugs swarming all around you,
        until you can't stand it any more. . . .
Then let Mary come to you.
Let her try to shoo the bugs away. . . .
        (But she cannot do it either!)

Then let her take you by the hand,
        moving slowly at first.
Soon the pace quickens
        and you move more cheerfully as you go along. . . .
You arrive at the top of the highest hill.
Feel the breeze on your face. . . .
Because you are up here, instead of down below,
        the bugs are gone;
        the gentle wind has conquered. . . .

Sit there, in silence. . . .
You are now freed from distempering distractions.
At last, you are able to hear the good news:
        You are able to rejoice, knowing the Lord is with you. . . .

Let Mary remind you how,
        in so many ways,
        this is already so. . . .

3

Freed From No-Good Worry

The angel said to her: "You shall conceive and shall bring forth a son, and you shall call his name Jesus. He shall be great . . . and of his kingdom there shall be no end." But Mary said, "How shall this happen, since I do not know man?" And the angel answered and said to her, "The Holy Spirit shall come upon you and the power of the Most High shall overshadow you . . . for nothing is impossible with God." And Mary said, "Behold the maidservant of God; let it be done to me according to your word."

Luke 1:30-38

Reflection

This is the last of the "Let Be" exercises preliminary to real prayer. Anxiety is as much a pest as discouragement. Holding on to the right to worry is as great an obstacle to grace as holding on to the right to be hurt.

We do, of course, have a right to worry. There are so many things that could go wrong, so many ways that they may not go right. How is one to know for sure?

We cannot know for sure. Too many uncertain things (including the free will of others) make the future unpredictable. Such a situation is unsatisfactory, and so we worry. We want to know what is in store for us before we risk committing ourselves. We want to believe that we can do a good job before we agree to start it. We get bogged down by forebodings about the future, as though we were

11

watching a tug of war waging in our brains: one side says, "I should do such and such;" then the other side draws us back, "But, on the other hand, it may not be a good idea because of this or that."

We get headaches from the "back and forth" of it. As a result, we end up exhausted, not doing anything.

With Mary, this was not the case. She gave herself over to the decision to "Let it be." She let go of her right to worry about future difficulties or the worrisome aspects attending anything unknown. She continued to be open to the present possibilities with God.

Nevertheless, it is interesting to think about how Mary might have responded if she had not disciplined herself against the warping effect of worry. If she were less self-controlled, she would have reacted to Gabriel's message with any number of "killer phrases" such as:

"What's the catch?"

"There may be terrible consequences in store for me: I may not be able to handle them!"

"On one hand, it seems good to agree to God's will; but on the other hand, it may cause me misery and over-excitement!"

"Ask God to get somebody else to do this job; my girl friend down the street could probably do it better than I!"

"I really don't think I'm qualified to be the mother of God. Let me think about it!"

She did nothing like that. She asked the one question that was necessary for her to know: "How can I be the mother of the Savior and still remain a virgin?" She was told. All else was left in God's hand. The divine plan of love would unfold, little by little, one day at a time. Mary was God's handmaid, trusting in the future that he would make for her. She let it be done, according to his word.

She will help us let it be, also. If only we invite her into our prayer, she will save us the trouble of wasting good energy with useless worries. She will replace anxiety with trust.

Prayer

In your imagination,
find a good room within a summer cottage—

one that is inaccessible to other people,
and free of telephones, television . . . and all inside noise. . . .

When you settle down,
think of some important steps in your future:
- a new career, perhaps
- what to do now that you have more time (or less time)
  on your hands
- whether or not to take responsibility
  for a deep love or friendship
- some other decisions which, if taken,
  will make your life quite different. . . .

Get two clean sheets of paper;
place them on the table in front of you. . . .
(At least, do this in your mind.)
On one page, write all the favorable reasons for the new venture. . . .
On the other page, list reasons against it. . . .

Now try this experiment:
(You've done this, perhaps many times, in real life.)
Bounce from one item on one page
to the opposing item on the other page,
        as though you were watching a ping-pong game:
        "On the one hand . . ." "But on the other hand . . ."
Get a headache from all this jostling in your mind. . . ."

Let Mary enter your room, now.
Let her urge you to stick to the list written on one sheet of paper . . .
        (Turn over the other sheet . . .)
She asks you to write down some more ideas on that page.
Perhaps she will add to your list some ideas of her own. . . .

Then both of you do the same with the other sheet. . . .

What feels best for you now?
What do your guts tell you?
What seems "right,"
        despite the worry that might be part of the decision?
Tell Mary about it, in your own words. . . .

Then let her tell you her story:

about all the things that puzzled her at the Annunciation. . . .
Let her assure you how well it all worked out,
   even though she was baffled at the time. . . .

And let her guide you into the same trust she had,
   urging you to let it be done to you, according to God's
      word. . . .

4

Problems in Need of Sleep

When Mary had been betrothed to Joseph . . . she was found to be
with child by the Holy Spirit. Joseph, her husband, being a just man,
and not wishing to expose her to reproach, was minded to put her
away privately. But while he thought on these things, behold, an angel
of the Lord appeared to him in a dream, saying, "Do not be afraid,
Joseph, son of David, to take Mary to be your wife; for that which is
begotten of her is of the Holy Spirit. . . ." So Joseph, arising from
sleep, did as the angel of the Lord had commanded him.

Matthew 1:18-24

Reflection

There is no grammatical symbol, in any language, that indicates a
time lapse. If the writer does not supply a clause such as "after three
days," "six months later," or something such as that, the reader must
either imagine long periods of waiting for the next thing to happen, or
assume that one experience followed immediately upon another.

Unfortunately, most people assume an "immediacy of
sequence" when they read the gospel passage above. One sentence
picks up where the other leaves off, without any qualifier of time.
Joseph had a problem. It was a problem of conscience. His fiance was
pregnant . . . and not by him. These were facts!

A quick reading of the passage sees Joseph with the problem,
wrestling with it for a few moments, deciding to renounce the
engagement with Mary. (But privately, so as not to be unduly harsh.)

Then, it would seem that Joseph went to bed. Apparently, as

soon as he hit the pillow, he fell asleep—the way a person sleeps who has no worry in the world. In his sleep, he had a dream. (Or, rather, the dream had him.) The dream revealed a message of divine assurance. Mary's pregnancy was all God's doing. It was for God's salvation purposes, his plan of love. Joseph would be needed in this plan of love. Relief at last. Doubts were healed. Love was restored, made more beautiful than before. The wedding was planned.

But it probably wasn't all that easy, because the resolution of the problem didn't happen that fast. It may have been months—at least a few weeks between one event and the other. If so (and likely so), these weeks would have been a time of great pain for both of them, caused by the bewilderment of it all.

Mary had to sit back and simply wait it out. She knew that her husband-to-be was hurt by two facts: 1) Obviously, she was going to have a baby. 2) Just as obviously, he had nothing to do with it.

She could see how upset he was. She could read the lines in his face, the slump of his shoulders, (perhaps) the shyness in her company during all that time. He didn't know what to do. She couldn't tell him how it happened; it was up to God to do so. God took the initiative with her. He would do the same with her husband. She just waited, while Joseph puzzled it out for himself.

Almost all of us, one way or another, have had to live out our versions of Mary's silent suffering. At times, we also are burdened by a secret we cannot share. A third person's integrity demands our silence. Yet, we can see how this silence hurts someone we love.

This is one kind of "silent powerlessness" in a situation. Another kind is even more universal, especially for parents, teachers, or people in the helping professions—concerning those times when we would so much want to help, but we can say or do nothing to relieve the hurt of someone we love. That person has to work it out on his or her own.

Days can seem very long under such circumstances. There is nothing we can do but wait, and pray.

Sometimes, in our prayers, we can ask Mary to be with us, to help us go through these demands for patience. She cannot take away the hurt that comes from a sense of powerlessness. (She could not take away her own hurt.) But she can assure us that it is right to hold on to our silence and be calm. And she can give us hope that, as it was with her, things may turn out better than they were before.

Prayer

In your imagination,
sit down by a table, on an outdoor patio . . .
one that has a beautiful view. . . .

You have prepared a delicious lunch
for Mary and Joseph and yourself.
(Try to guess what kind of food they would like. . . .)
You have all this ready. . . .

They arrive.
Greet one another in whatever way seems right. . . .
Imagine the small talk as you eat lunch.
(Do not stay too long with this.
Just feel the mood of it; let it be delightful. . . .)

After lunch, ask Mary to tell you
about the "waiting time"
between the Annunciation and Joseph's dream. . . .
Let her tell you, in her own words, about how she managed;
        and what her feelings were. . . .

Then let Joseph tell you how grateful he was
        because his wife did not try to rush things . . .
        but gave him time to work out his problem for himself. . . .

Finally, let them both advise you how to manage
        as you are patiently waiting
        for those you love
        to take responsibility for their own decisions. . . .

5

Your Own Magnificat

Mary arose and went in haste . . . and greeted Elizabeth. . . . Elizabeth was filled with the Holy Spirit and cried out with a loud voice, saying, "Blessed are you among women and blessed is the fruit of your womb. . . . And blessed is she who has believed, because the things promised her by the Lord shall be accomplished." And Mary said, "My soul magnifies the Lord, and my spirit rejoices in God my Savior. . . ."

Luke 1:39-46

Reflection

A premonition of sorrow was mixed in with the other joyful mysteries of Mary. But the overall mood of Mary's visit with Elizabeth must have been pure joy—before, during, and after.

It was good to be able to do something for a friend. After all this waiting for God to prepare his work of love, and waiting for her term of pregnancy (and, perhaps, still waiting for Joseph to have his dream)—all this was draining. So it was good to be active, and Elizabeth needed her. God's message implied as much. She went.

Even anticipating the visit must have been a joyful experience. (It is fascinating how both women were such good models of the art of listening.) Mary had a marvelous story that she must have been just bursting to tell someone. So did her cousin. That a woman is having her first baby is newsworthy enough. But that each one is pregnant under such amazing circumstances is even more telling. There is even more need to celebrate the event by sharing the whole story with an understanding friend.

Yet each cousin deferred to the other—each was prepared to be a good listener, rather than a good storyteller. Mary simply greeted Elizabeth. She gave her cousin the chance to speak first. Elizabeth did. But she, too, was deferential. She did not start talking about her child, or her good news. All her message was given over to praise of Mary and of her child.

How good they were to one another. Elizabeth proclaimed the greatness of her cousin, the "blessed one among all women." Mary did not demur. No false humility in her response. No downgrading of her cousin's praise, or denying of her magnificence. Mary was great. For she had already begun the process of making God great (and making him better known and better loved) by the good use of the gifts God gave her.

False pride was as far from her as false humility. There was no doubt about where her greatness came from. All was from God. She sang her Magnificat of joy and expansive exaltation: "I magnify the Lord; I rejoice in God my Savior."

The song continued. Once Mary honored God for the greatness that was given her, she went on to sing of history. She gathered in, with sweeping statements, many of God's "Ways of Greatness" in the past; and then went on to foretell what can be expected in the future. All the *anawim* of the world (the poor, the downcast, the out of luck, the powerless) have always been treated by God in his topsy-turvy way. Ultimately, the humbled become magnificent; the proud are humbled.

Mary sang about how God had changed her from a "nobody" to a most highly favored "somebody." Her experience then embraced all time. She improvised a kind of "class song" for all the classless people of the world: all of the oppressed, the exploited, the ignored.

"Blessed are the poor; they will be comforted." Mary's Magnificat anticipated Christ's beatitudes by thirty years. It must have been a moving experience for Mary to understand this with such a sure instinct and to proclaim it with such conviction.

For both women, the days spent after these precious moments of greeting must have been joyful, too. There was time for a long visit. They had the leisure to poke into God's possibilities. Perhaps they made conjectures about what these astonishing events would mean for them in the years to come.

They could see themselves as signal bearers for everyone who is despised or dejected in any way. They would always be "standards for liberation," enabling exploited classes and dehumanized individuals to sing their own Magnificat.

And for those of us who are subject to more ordinary kinds of desolation, they would be the models for every prayerful person who needs a visit from good friends, every now and then, to keep his or her courage up.

Prayer

In your imagination,
get into your routine of feeling "small,"
feeling like you are "nothing but a nobody". . . .
(This comes from the particular ways you are most sensitive
to being ignored, or put down, by others.)
Feel this, strongly, once again. . . .

Then prepare to visit a person you know
who seems to have the same qualities as Elizabeth:
a good listener;
kind, warm, affectionate;
someone who is able to see the good in you,
and bring this out. . . .

Your friend is waiting for you
in a quiet place where you have met before. . . .
Mary is there, also. . . .
Take some time to be present at this scene. . . .

Let your friend praise you for your goodness.
(Do not resist the compliments.
Joyfully accept them.
Try to appreciate what your friend appreciates in you.
Spend as much time as you can,
letting this praise sink in. . . .)

Then let Mary help you "sing your Magnificat."
Let her show you that all your good qualities
are gifts from God.

Let her teach you how to be grateful for your greatness:
    greatness already achieved,
    and greatness possible. . . .

And let her guide you so that you, too,
can identify with the poor and the handicapped. . . .
Let her suggest ways that you can help them,
    as she and your friend helped you. . . .

6

A Nativity in Every Love

And it came to pass . . . that the days for her to be delivered were fulfilled. And [Mary] brought forth her son and wrapped him in swaddling clothes and laid him in a manger.

Luke 2:6-7

And the Word was made flesh and dwelt among us.

John 1:14

Reflection

The issue of Christmas was love, on a large scale and on a small scale—both larger and smaller than we usually visualize it. The scale was small because it was just one person who brought forth the Word made flesh. It was one individual mother: localized by one small mountain town, speaking one dialect, praying in one style of prayer, having one set of feast days and fast days. For thirty years, Jesus would be bound by the customs and colloquialisms of Mary and Joseph, and their families and their neighborhood.

But the issuing forth was also much larger than Christmas cards imply. December 25 usually provides us with but a snapshot of love—a peek at the creche. The reality of it was more like a movie, with complex dynamics already at work.

When Mary brought Jesus to birth we could say, quite literally,

"The child has his mother's eyes." There was no human father in this case. The "flesh" of eyesight was a gift on Mary's part.

In every birth, "flesh" indicates all the physical and psychic endowments that parents give their babies. But flesh is even more than that. By means of Mary's gift, God took flesh of all that made Mary who she was. He took up his mother's memories—memories of her own parents, and of the stories they had told her. In Nazereth, God was "fleshed" by his mother's unique way of preparing food and by her preferences for certain passages of Sacred Scripture. The Second Person of the Blessed Trinity was formed by Mary's way of making friends and telling stories and laughing at the things that struck her as funny. The Word of God pronounced human words as he was taught by Mary. God learned to have pet phrases, and learned to love a special fig tree in back of where he lived, and felt the pleasure of shade in the late afternoon, and found out that homemade soup was good for him . . . because all these, and much more, were various aspects of the gift of Mary's flesh.

We know, to some degree, how Mary must have felt . . . as she slowly discovered the gift of herself taking root in the child of her womb. The dynamic consequences involved in "giving flesh to love" is the same with every human. We have all marveled at how many things are "part of the package" when love is allowed to issue between two friends. In some way, we see our life—all the parts of our life that make up our condition and our personality—become our friend's life too. Our friend does the same with us . . . even to certain pet phrases that sneak into each other's vocabulary. In every true friendship, something develops that is a kind of "nativity."

Of course, when God was born, Jesus did not become a carbon copy of his mother. But just the same, he was nurtured and conditioned by everything that Mary knew, loved, talked about, and cared for.

So it is, in a lesser sense, with every friendship issuing forth a new life, born of the life that has been given to each other.

Because of Mary's motherhood, in all its complexity, she can help us understand how precious is the gift we give to others and receive from them. Because she has had such a good experience, she can be our "midwife" as we continue to give birth to the love of God and the love of others. Whether we are men or women, she can help us with our "motherhoods," in whatever way they happen.

Prayer

In your imagination,
go to an old-fashioned room,
in an old-fashioned house. . . .
It has a high ceiling, pure white.
You are half sitting, half lying on a comfortable lounge chair.
Mary is beside you, on one just like it. . . .

Imagine that you see the famous painting in the Sistine Chapel:
the Creator-God is touching the finger of Adam.
(Just slightly touching, fingertip to fingertip.)
God is nurturing man by his creative contact:
    giving Adam the qualities of love, wisdom, free will,
    capacity to be grateful. . . .
Stay with this scene as long as it seems good to do so. . . .
Then let Mary tell you what she sees in it. . . .

Now imagine a new painting on the ceiling:
See Mary in Bethlehem
at the very moment that she touched the index finger of her baby
for the first time. . . .
Think of what her feelings might have been. . . .
Then tell her about what came to you in prayer. . . .

Let Mary add to your ideas,
    filling in the picture
    with some of the particulars that only she could know. . . .

Now think of two or three people you love
    whose friendship you cherish;
    who have given you a part of their life,
    and have allowed you to give them a part of yours. . . .
Understand this love and friendship
to be something like the Creator-God
    giving life to Adam;
and something like the Blessed Mother
    giving life to Jesus. . . .

Imagine your index fingers
    tenderly and slowly touching one another. . . .
Let your love flow from you into them. . . .

Finally, let Mary teach you better
    about the fatherhood of friendship
    and the motherhood of love. . . .
And let her guide you into more gratitude for your "nativities"
    when you gave to others
    the best of the life that was in you. . . .

7

Laws That Give Thanks

And when the days of [Mary's] purification were fulfilled according to
the Law of Moses, they took [Jesus] up to Jerusalem to present him to
the Lord—as it is written in the Law of the Lord . . . and to offer a
sacrifice according to what is said in the Law of the Lord. . . .

Luke 2:22-24

Reflection

Three times, within two sentences, St. Luke tells us that Mary and
Joseph presented Jesus to God "according to the Law." The evangelist seems to be going out of his way to show that the Holy Family
was law-abiding.

Laws and customs are usually considered restrictions, limiting
individual spontaneity. But this is one-sided. A regimen of action—a
"way in which we do things"—is, more often than not, something
that is freeing for the individual, not supressing.

Havoc would result if there were no laws such as speed limits
for traffic, or punishment for anti-social conduct. There would be no
security anywhere, without the law. There would be no stability
without certain customs that influence the way we act.

Language is a "law" of sorts. Tradition has dictated to the next
generation that "These things are called chairs; these are called meat;

these, vegetables; this, salt; that, pepper . . . and so on." No individual can change the words around and expect to be understood.

Likewise, each person has developed a number of "laws within," which are self-trained habits of acting. These "cultivated instincts" free the person for more important pursuits. We would go crazy if we had to concentrate every time we tied our shoes, brushed our teeth, or used a knife and fork. Consider the routine of getting up in the morning. Thank God we don't have to be deliberate about each detail. We'd have no energy left for the rest of the day if we did not put some of our activities on "automatic pilot," complying with the "laws" of our built-in habits of behavior.

Laws provide the relish in another area of our lives, too. Consider all of our traditions: the family, religious and national customs. Certain things are done so that "we as a family" or "we as Christians" or "we as Americans" celebrate special occasions such as Thanksgiving, Easter, different anniversaries, or Christmas. Through these customs, especially on Christmas, we bake certain foods in certain ways, or decorate the tree with certain treasures of the past, or exchange gifts at certain times with special rituals, or honor other customs which have been cherished by family history.

None of these activities restrict our freedom. They are established customs and defined patterns of acting through which we are able to do what we want to do. They are, for the most part, regulations determining how we are to remember our reasons to be grateful—to our family, to our country, to our God. As such, they are liberating and assuring, giving us prepared occasions for expressing our love "in style."

This is how it was with Mary and Joseph. Of course, they were not strictly bound by the law to present their son to God. Their son already belonged to God. Yet, it was good to obey the law anyway. It was a marvelous opportunity for Joseph to repeat the obedience he gave God when he agreed to love and support his family. It was a good way for Mary to affirm, once more, her willingness to "let it be done, according to God's will."

It is a healing experience to take a positive look at our laws, customs, and traditions. Not all laws should be uncritically accepted. Some customs (even the customs of language and family traditions) can become strait jackets to creativity and fresh enthusiasms. But only when we learn to love what is beneficial about the behavior patterns that we have been trained to perform can we sift out the unnecessary and/or the ignoble aspects of such training.

It would be a healing prayer experience for us to go to Mary, who is the freest of all God's creatures, and ask her to help us put a personal spirit of gratitude back into the general rules that tell us how to worship God in an orderly way.

Prayer

In your imagination,
go back to the home where you grew up. . . .

Let memory take you back to your childhood:
it is a few days after Christmas,
during one of the happiest years you had,
between age six and twelve. . . .

With your adult mind
recollect all the laws and customs
that made this Christmas so delightful:
- the family traditions;
- the particular way your parish worshipped God;
- the things your family did that put a
    "particular style" in the way you celebrated. . . .
Stay with these good memories for a while. . . .

Let Mary sit down beside you.
Let her tell you of her joy as she obeyed the Laws of the Lord. . . .
And let her approve of your ways,
    your traditions. . . .

Then let Mary take you on an imaginary tour,
stopping at special places, and special times,
    during the year to come.
Let her talk to you about certain birthdays coming up,
    and anniversaries and national observances;
How each occasion is such a good opportunity
to give thanks to others in a tangible way. . . .

Also, let Mary invest you with a genuine spirit of piety
—a love for religion that she had—

so that every Sunday
and all the feast days of the church
will give you a desire to fulfill the law of praise:
    because they are occasions
    for presenting God
    with your freely given gratitude
    for all that you have, and are, and hope to be. . . .

8

Dominoes of Grief

There was in Jerusalem a man named Simeon, and this man was just and devout . . . And he came by inspiration of the Spirit into the temple . . . and he received [Jesus] into his arms and blessed God . . . (Then) Simeon . . . said to Mary his mother, "Behold, this child is destined for the fall and for the rise of many in Israel, and for a sign that shall be contradicted. And your own soul a sword shall pierce, that the thoughts of many hearts may be revealed.

Luke 2:25-35

Reflection

Everyone has a certain set of sorrows, as unique to the individual as fingerprints. There is always one greatest sorrow, looming larger than the others. But all the sorrows, coming before and after the great one, are experienced almost as sensitively because any one can set off a "chain reaction" influenced by all the others.

Mary was no exception. Perhaps her greatest sorrow was standing by the cross. Perhaps it was something else. Whatever it was, it was linked with the first one that we know about.

It happened just forty days after Christ was born. Soon after Mary presented her son to God, an old man took the infant in his arms and predicted that Jesus would meet violent contradiction (the symbol was "sword") and Mary would be heart-pierced . . . almost heartbroken.

Mary must have felt the pain of such a prophecy. The blood probably drained from her face: her hand trembled slightly, longing to take her son back into her arms and protect him. But, no matter how terrible the first shock was, it would be felt even more deeply as the years continued . . . when she would see the destiny unfold, little by little. The whole accumulation would add to what she felt at the presentation in the temple, making the memory of Simeon's words all the more real, all the more poignant.

Everybody, one way or another, has experienced such a chain reaction caused by sorrow. It seems that joys do not elicit the same mood. Each joy is felt, usually, as a particular phenomenon. It does not "spark" a memory of other joys felt in the past, or inaugurate a presentiment of joys that will come in the future.

Sorrows, however, seem to do just that. Consequently, it is very difficult to get out of a "down" mood; and it is also difficult to help others get out of theirs. It is not so easy to isolate the cause of a depression, or understand why a particular hurt is so painful. Grief does not come from a single incident. It is often fed by remembrance of many other experiences . . . and it feeds a foreboding of more sorrows waiting to overtake us later.

In the case of Simeon's prophecy, the event, of itself, was not a sorrow. It was a prediction of what lay ahead. Just the same, this incident may have energized a remembrance of "swords of contradiction" that Mary had already experienced. We know nothing of the Mother of God prior to her annunciation. We do not know her early life. But the context of Mary's presentation of her son in the temple was: 1) obedience to the law, and 2) the desire to please God in every way possible.

These two qualities may have caused her many turns of unhappiness before. Certain children are always jealous, and they often retaliate vindictively when one of their peers gets high marks in school or shows them up in virtue.

Mary could not have escaped such petty jealousies. This means that, even at fifteen years old, she already knew what it meant to be the cause of envious contention and to suffer put-downs from her friends and to feel the loneliness of being left out.

Now she heard that there would be many more sorrows, even worse than those she had already known. She and Jesus would continue to be unaccepted by many people, and she would be hated by those "many in Israel" who would back up their hatred by cruel deeds.

There could be no escape from it. Obedience to God's plan of love was paramount. The passion would follow from this determination to obey God's will. Simeon was sure of it. So was Mary.

Sorrows do have a cumulative effect. But so does every act of love. Mary, having experienced them both, can help us develop a constancy in love even as we feel the falling dominoes of sorrow—which have been set off by the stroke of some sword of contradiction.

Prayer

As a detached observer of yourself,
remember the last time your feelings were hurt:
- when you were neglected by friends;
- overlooked;
- made to feel that your were "the enemy" somehow.

(In your recollections, choose only those experiences
that were not caused by anything wrong that you did.
They came from other people's thoughtlessness or spite. . . .)
Feel the hurt of it again.

Now, return to the first time in your life
when something similar happened to you:
- maybe it was your parents who hurt you
- maybe a teacher
- maybe your friends in school.
Understand how much the same your feelings were. . . .
There is a bond of grief
between the first and last experiences. . . .

Recall, also, some of the in-between times
when something similar happened. . . .
Try to locate the particular way in which your "chain of sorrow"
hits you.

In your imagination,
go to a favorite place where you sometimes lick your wounds.
Let Mary join you there.
Let her explain, in her own words,
how she knows about your sword of sorrow,
and the cumulative effect of each new sadness. . . .

Let her comfort you, console you. . . .
These hurts cannot be helped.
There will always be mean-hearted people in your life . . .
But let her encourage you with fresh determination
to stay true to your version
        of Mary's obedience,
And to be constant in your gift of love, no matter what. . . .

9

Goodness In, Goodness Out

There was also Anna . . . She was of great age . . . with fasting and prayers worshipping night and day. And coming up at that very hour, she began to give praise to the Lord, and spoke of him to all who were awaiting the redemption of Jerusalem.

Luke 2:36-38

Reflection

The computers of today can give us a thought-provoking insight into the lovely, gentle, almost wordless event that happened to Mary, twenty centuries ago.

There is a saying among computer engineers: Gigo: "Garbage in; garbage out." That is, if you put inconsequential information into the computer, you won't get anything but nonsense out of it.

The monks of the Middle Ages understood the wisdom of this slogan. Monks were obliged to be faithful to *Lectio Divina,* or "Divine Study": the reading of Sacred Scripture and other books that wrote about God and moral virtue. The idea was that, if the monk "fed" his head and heart with good reading, chances were that wisdom and goodness would come out of his head and heart. It would be a case of "Goodness in; goodness out."

Such a slogan still has practical applications. Filling our minds with good reading is not only a value in itself. It also has a "replacement value"; it means we won't be filling our minds with garbage.

Many people "Gigo" the computers of their brains with television trivia, gossip of the streets, fantasies homespun by idleness, or saps to the imagination spoon-fed by movies and trashy fiction.

It is no wonder that so much garbage comes out of so many people's mouths. That garbage has been the constant diet of their brain's intake.

With Anna the prophetess, there was no room for garbage. She had prayed and fed her prayer with Sacred Scripture for most of her very long life. So when the time came for her to speak about serious things, she possessed a mind that was uncluttered, a heart that was non-trivialized. She could understand the true significance of this marvelous baby in his mother's arms—her instincts had not been "overdosed" by incidental tugs at her attention.

Mary was so pleased to hear Anna praise her child. Anna was not just anybody. Her praise counted more than the gushy compliments of the village gossips. There was the conviction of wisdom that accompanied Anna's response. She carried an assurance which only a prayerful person can put to words.

Anna's statements were all the more precious to Mary because they followed Simeon's dire prediction about the cutting edge of sorrow. The consoling sun came out to push away (for the present) all the menacings of storm. In a sense, Mary read her own *Lectio Divina* by listening to the words of Anna. The wise old woman was a holy person—holy in the sense of "wholeness," or "not lacking a capacity to understand," "not torn apart by distractions." She was one of the many good people who fed Mary's heart. Joseph, Elizabeth, Zachary, many more . . . all helped to keep alive her trust in God. Their presence to her were like good books. By wise words and by the example of their lives, they gave Mary more material to ponder, over and over, in her heart.

Prayer

Bring to mind your favorite saint.
Remember the first time you read, or heard,
    about this saint. . . .
Try to bring back the feelings you had
    when you first resonated so intensely to your hero. . . .

Also, recall two wise old persons in your life:
a man and a woman
    who have helped you by their words
    or simply by their presence, their wordless kindness. . . .

Think of these three people. . . .
(They are to you what Anna was to Mary.)
Enjoy the memory of them once again. . . .

In your imagination,
go to a quiet place where all of you can be comfortable. . . .
Let Mary join you there. . . .
Let her praise your friends, each of them,
    for the goodness that they are in themselves;
    and for their good influence on you. . . .
(Mary may tell you things about them
that you never knew before. . . .)

Then let all four—whoever wants to—
help you with your *Lectio Divina,*
    your "goodness in" so that "goodness may come out". . . .

Let them warn you against certain superficial things
it would be better not to watch or read. . . .
(Things which may be blunting your senses
    and cluttering your mind. . . .)
Then let them advise you about worthwhile reading
and people of good will and stimulating interests
    it would be better to draw from. . . .

At the end, let them say goodbye
in whatever way they want to. . . .
And see them out the door
    (perhaps with a promise to visit you again . . .).

10

Pulling Up Roots

An angel of the Lord appeared in a dream to Joseph, saying, "Arise, and take the child and his mother, and flee into Egypt, and remain there until I tell you. . . . Then Herod . . . was angry and he sent [his soldiers] and slew all the boys in Bethlehem and all its neighborhoods who were two years old or under. . . .

Matthew 2:13-16

Reflection

Perhaps the best way to appreciate both the sorrow and the steadfastness of Mary and Joseph is to see them in the context of a "crunch of consequences" with which we can identify because we have experienced something similar in our own lives. We, too, have pulled up stakes, left family and friends, and gone off to a new place and/or a new destiny.

We went off, but what happened to those we left behind? And how do we suppose they might be thinking about us, now that we left them behind? Do they resent our decision? Have they turned bitter against us? How are they taking it since—let's be honest about it—they were more or less "jilted"?

For instance, when two people marry, by this decision they each say "I have chosen not to marry all the other friends I had been dating." How do these ex'es feel, since they were less preferred? How do parents feel when a son or daughter enters priesthood or the religious life (and these parents were hoping to have grandchildren)? How does the family feel when a young adult leaves for a job that will make homecoming a rare occurrence? Is the family resentful, perhaps outraged, by what they interpret as a geographical slap in the face?

Other instances may come up in middle age. Maybe a husband decides to take on a second job or a time consuming hobby (and his wife does not like the empty chair at supper time). Maybe his wife decides to have a second career, or go back to school (and her husband complains about the disruption of his routine). Sometimes a spouse finds married life to be so intolerable that it ends with a separation or divorce (and the rest of the family take it personally, as an insult to them—an intolerable dislocation of the person who had provided them with normal expectations).

Take these few examples as "metaphors of understanding," giving us some notion of what must have been going on in the minds of Mary and Joseph soon after the birth of Christ. They obeyed a dream. They "pulled up stakes." They left abruptly without a word to their aunts, uncles, and cousins of the House of David, Bethlehem.

They knew their decision would not be understood. Resentment (for some families of Bethlehem, virulent bitterness) would be the "crunch of consequences" lingering on in the neighborhood they left. Some of their relatives had seen their infant boys butchered before their eyes. No matter what a detached observer might say—"It wasn't Mary's fault your child was murdered; it was Herod who did it"—they would still insist, with hatred in their eyes, "If it weren't for Mary's child, our child would not have died!" Undoubtedly, they would hate the holy family even more for "running out on them."

It had to be a lingering sorrow for many, many years. Mary and Joseph had placed themselves under obedience to the will of God. The flight into Egypt was part of his will, so they did it. They adapted to new circumstances as best they could. They got on with the job of a new daily routine, living faithfully to God and being true to themselves—despite changed surroundings and despite the hurts they caused others by their move.

The Holy Family can be a traveling guide for us when important decisions cause us to leave the people and things we had grown familiar with. And they can be a comfort when this decision is resented by those we left behind, in our version of "Bethlehem."

Prayer

In your imagination,
place yourself under the shade of some palm trees,
in an oasis ridged by desert all around. . . .

Think of the distance you have traveled
since you made the decision to pull up roots,
        in whatever way you did so. . . .
Consider the repercussions it caused
among those people you are no longer associated with. . . .
Feel again:
        – the hurt in your heart because they don't understand
        – your sense of loss, because you don't have
                the comfort and security of what used to be
        – your wonder, sometimes, whether you made a mistake
        – and whatever else fits into the consequences
                coming from your decision. . . .

Quietly, the holy family joins you in your oasis.
They are going to Egypt.
They stop for a cool drink of water, and a chat. . . .
Mary asks you what you have been thinking about.
Tell her about your decision to move
        and tell her about some of your sorrows, too. . . .
        (All the courage and all the "crunch" of it—
        tell her about these things, in your own words. . . .)

Then let her tell you her story, and her feelings,
as she and Joseph took flight into Egypt. . . .
Finally, let her advise you how to pray for steadfastness;
and how to stay strong. . . .
Let her encourage you to keep working for
        greater purity of intention—
        so that you do not become selfish,
        or bitter
        in your new place. . . .

11

Growing Different Gracefully

When Jesus was twelve years old, [he and his parents] went up to Jerusalem according to the custom of the feast. And after they had fulfilled the days . . . the boy Jesus remained in Jerusalem, and his parents did not know it. . . . And after three days, they found him . . . and when they saw him, they were astonished. And his mother said to him, "Son, why have you done this to us? Behold your father and I have been seeking you in sorrow." And he said to them, "Why did you seek me? Did you not know that I must be about my Father's business?" But they did not understand . . . and Mary kept all these things carefully in her heart. . . .

Luke 2:41-52

Reflection

The flight into Egypt meant taking leave of others; the Holy Family had moved away from Bethlehem. The finding of Jesus in the temple meant (in a sense) taking leave of self. Both involved a leave-taking; but the second kind is more involved.

When Jesus was twelve years old, according to Jewish custom, he could already be considered "initiated" into adulthood. Taking charge of his own life, he remained in his Father's house. He began to be personally responsible for his "Father's business." Mary and Joseph knew nothing about this. They lost their son for three days. But more to the point, they lost their "little boy" forever. They also lost the concept of themselves as "parents of their little boy." This was one of the many passages through life that Mary and Joseph had to submit to . . . just as everyone does.

Getting born is the first of these passages. For nine months, we enjoy the peace and security of our mother's womb. Then out we go . . . and it is scary. Life has suddenly become much more complex, more fraught with fears, more insecure.

Soon afterward comes the next demand for change: as a child we must graduate from walking on all fours to standing on two legs. This also has fears attached to it. At first, we are so clumsy. We sense the risk of falling down, and we feel all the difficulties of apprenticeship. Later, of course we are glad we learned the art of walking, but at the time it wasn't easy.

And so it is with all the changes in our lives. Our early childhood gives way to school years. These, in turn, phase out into the world of work. In every stage, there is a kind of "dying" to the old so that we may give birth to the new. More often than not, there is a frightening sense of alienation attached to the process. The initial reaction can be negative—we feel unglued because the "stickum" by which we had put our lives together, the normal routines we had grown accustomed to, have all deserted us.

Mary must have experienced something of this. We tend to think that Mary's sorrow was losing Jesus for a while. It was. She admitted as much: "Your father and I were grieving . . . we were anxious and worried about you."

But this was only a temporary loss. The permanent loss was that of the person she was before she had found her son. Certainly, she already knew that Jesus would be a sword of contradiction . . . and that sorrow would pierce her heart. But Simeon's words were only a prediction. And anyway, that had happened twelve years ago. Mary had all those years to grow accustomed to being an ordinary wife and mother in a small village of Galilee.

Twelve years is a long time to get used to a certain way of life. Then, like an unexpected thunderclap, she was told that her ordinary routine would be totally lost to her some day. She now knew, hearing it from her twelve year old (with a force more poignant than hearing it from Simeon), that she must prepare to be a most extrordinary mother of a most amazing son . . . who would be about his Father's business—cleansing the temple and purifying hearts as the suffering servant of the world.

Exactly how Mary experienced the darkness and fear that was a part of this new challenge, we do not know. St. Luke only gives us a hint of it in the cryptic conclusion of this part of the gospel: "Mary kept all these things carefully in her heart."

Then eighteen years are shrouded in silence. We do not know how Mary kept these things carefully in her heart. But it was a time of growth for her. It had to be. She must have felt the stress as she let go of her early motherhood and pondered about what her new-found motherhood would be. She was different now, because she was the parent of a maturing son. She moved her life up a notch.

Because she "knows the territory" so well, she can guide us through the perils of our passages in life. She can help us "grow different" gracefully. All we have to do is ask.

Prayer

In your imagination,
return to your mother's womb.
You are just about to be born into the world. . . .

Pretend that you are already equipped
with all the mental and emotional faculties you have now.
How would you feel in such a situation?
Consider what you would leave:
> – the womb is a cozy place, never too hot or cold
> – it gives complete assurance that you will never
>   be hungry
> – you will never be left alone
> – you are protected, secure. . . .

Then some instinct calls you to abandon this paradise
for a new life situation. . . .
What would strike you immediately?
Would you not be reluctant to leave?
(In fact, did you not cry when you actually did leave?)
Think of your birthing in this way. . . .

Then pile into this, all the other times
you had to change the way you live. . . .

Feel once again the tension of it:
    – the desire to hang on to what you have
    – the strangeness and loneliness
        of the new world you are being pushed into. . . .
Let them all be a part of one experience,
leaving the secure world for one that is more complex. . . .

Now allow yourself to sense Mary's presence.
(She has been beside you, somehow, during all this time.)

Let her teach you that you must grow.
You cannot stagnate.
You must take risks, even if grief comes with the risks. . . .
You must be willing to let go of controls over your life
    so that you may live life
    in a richer, more demanding way. . . .

Finally, let her show you how you have already grown
because of the risks you have taken.
And let her give you hope
by which you can look forward to challenges in the future. . . .

And let her pray for you
so that you will focus on trust in God
    rather than on fear of the unknown. . . .
As you ponder how God has guided you so far,
    keeping his love carefully in your heart. . . .

PART TWO

Mary
With Jesus in
His Teens and Twenties

12

Refreshment With Christ

"Jerusalem, Oh Jerusalem [if only you would let me . . .] how often would I have gathered your children together, as a hen gathers her young under her wings . . ."

Luke 13:34

"Come to me all you who labor and are burdened and I will refresh you . . . I will give you rest."

Matthew 11:28

Reflection

Even though the infancy narratives insist quite strongly to the contrary, many Christians still feel that Jesus was a kind of Superman who arrived one day from heaven (something like "the planet Krypton") fully grown and fully equipped for the conquering of evil and the doing of good.

Because the gospels tell us next to nothing about the hidden years of our Lord, we sometimes think it best to let it go at that, lest we contrive new narratives of Jesus and give him a resumé that was never intended. We are warned against thinking about his hidden life because any such specualtion would make Christ into a teenage wonderworker . . . or, in some spectacular way, set him apart as being drastically different from other children.

But prayer does not have to neglect consideration of those unrecorded years. True prayer will not turn Jesus into someone that he was not. It will simply give a fuller sense of our Lord's maturing process.

St. Luke encapsulates three decades of life in two brief passages:

> [When Jesus was forty days old] his parents took him back to Galilee, to their own town of Nazareth. Meanwhile, the child grew to maturity, and he was filled with wisdom; and God's favor was with him. (Luke 2:39-40).

> [When Jesus was twelve years old] he went down with his parents to Nazareth and lived under their authority. His mother stored up all these things in her heart. And Jesus increased in wisdom, in stature, and in favor with God and men. (Luke 2:51-52).

Thus the Word of God was made flesh by more than Mary's womb. He was also "fleshed" by Mary's authority over his growing years, by her and Joseph's parental care, by the neighbors he grew up with, and by the familiar ways in which every human grows into maturity.

Although we are given only two brief summaries in Luke's gospel, we do know certain spontaneous statements Jesus made after he began the years of his known ministry. These can be considered hints, providing us with good guesses about how the child grew in wisdom, stature, and good favor.

Certain specifics may be suggested, tentatively. They will not be helpful for scholarship, but they may be helpful for prayer. Perhaps the best way to make these suggestions is by way of parables:

> The reign of God may be likened to a little boy who became very frightened by a thunderstorm that came down suddenly from Mount Carmel into his village of Galilee. He shivered with fear from the sound of it, and from the way it shook his house and the trees outside.

Then he ran to his mother. She understood at once. She took him on her lap, hugged him, and while rocking him back and forth, told him the story of a mother hen who gathered her chicks under her wing. Little by little, she made them warm from the cold and comforted from their fears of the world outside.

Soon the little boy was asleep in his mother's arms.

After this experience, the little boy always wanted to hear the same story whenever he was troubled and afraid.

Then, one day after he grew up, he was searching his mind for a story to tell people how much he wanted to be a person whom they could trust. He thought of his childhood and linked himself with the mother hen. Like her with her chicks, he would give people such a sense of security that they would never again have to be afraid, or be at war, or dread anything.

And so he told his story . . . because his mother had given birth to his words by the story she told him long ago.

Here is another parable:

The reign of God is like a man in his late teens who was once hired to work in the vineyards. He worked all day under the hot sun. Fellow laborers were complaining all the time. They were mean to one another; they played cruel tricks on the young man. It was a miserable day.

After the work was over, he observed that many of the workers did not want to go home. They didn't even want to think about facing their family's criticism of their meager paycheck.

He marveled. Unlike them, he really looked forward to going home. His parents provided him with a place of refreshment, joy, and peace. He could rest there. It was always good to relax with them. It was restorative and comfortable.

Then this young man lived another ten years or so, and he began his public ministry. He invited disciples to join him, assuring them—and all who labor and are burdened—that he would refresh them and give them rest . . . as his mother had done for him when he got home. . . .

Such parables were probably never spoken by our Lord. We

only know about two metaphors he used, which were really "compressed parables." They told all people, for all time: 1) "You can trust me as little chickens trust their mother." 2) "You can count on me to be a haven of refreshment, where you can rest from labor and lay your burdens down."

But the metaphors came from somewhere. It is possible that Mary was personally responsible for both of them. It is possible that she herself was the "parable" behind her son's realization of himself.

It does make sense. But perhaps it makes more sense in an atmosphere of prayer than in the suggestions of psychological inference.

Prayer

In your memory,
think of all your burdens and worries
that you have accumulated for the last few years. . . .

Imagine these as heavy packages, weighing on your shoulders.
With this heaviness, you are walking, alone, uphill,
        on an unfamiliar dirt road. . . .
You are tired.
It begins to rain;
        then it becomes pelting rain, mixed with hail.
You are frightened by the storm, are soaked to the skin. . . .

Then you see the light of a fire, some way off the road.
You are relieved.
Light is the sign of life. . . .
You come upon a blazing fire.
There is food cooking in a pot. . . .
Behind it is a well-built lean-to.

Jesus is there; he has been waiting for you.
He removes the burdens from your shoulders,
provides you with dry clothes,
feeds you with the stew that has been cooking on the fire. . . .
        Take time to enjoy the good feeling of being restored.

Soon the storm has passed . . .
The sun is shining.

Let Jesus tell you, in his own way,
how his mother relieved him of his fears and worries
    when he was young;
and how he looked forward to going home
    after a hard day's work.

Finally, let him invite you to himself:
    so that you may trust him even more than you do now
    when you are burdened and upset . . .
And let him suggest how you can be
a "place of refreshment and peace" for others
    as he always is for you—
        —as Mary and Joseph were for him, in Nazareth.

13

Good Teaching Methods

And in many such parables [Jesus] spoke the word to them, accordingly as they were able to understand it. Without parables he did not speak to them, but privately he explained all things to his disciples.

Mark 4:33-34

Jesus said, "Come to me . . . and learn of me [that is, enter my school] for I am meek . . ."

Matthew 11:28

Reflection

A commonplace principle of pedagogy goes something like this: When we are at our best, in any kind of teaching situation, we are somewhat reflecting the way our favorite teachers have taught us.

The teaching situation is to be interpreted broadly, to mean any "helping others by means of words." It includes parents with their children; educators and coaches at school or camp; ministers of the Word of God; counselors, psychiatrists, supervisors in all lines of work . . . even a friend giving advice to a friend.

In all these cases, the way in which we teach (or counsel or advise) is partly an imitated extension of the people who have taught us. It is not, of course, a carbon copy. We have taken the teaching style of our best mentors and made them our own. Even so, there are similarities. The way we guide others is, to some extent, modeled after those who guided us. There is a mixture: part of our teaching method is copied from past models, part of it is uniquely our own.

Thus it was with Jesus. His "style" and his authority were certainly unique to him. The crowds continually marveled that "Nobody has taught the way that he does!"

Yet there also was a certain stamp of similarity left on him by those who guided his steps. When he urged the people to "learn of me" (or "enroll in my school") Jesus was contrasting his teaching style with the method of his contemporaries, the Pharisees. When he characterized himself as being meek, he was lining himself up with the prophets of Sacred Scripture who were approachable, not stiff or overbearing. The teachers of the Old Testament were always sensitive to the learning capacities of their audience. From Moses to the authors of the Wisdom Literature, they were practical guides of spiritual growth. They were homespun, not demanding or haughty or "fancy worded," as were many of the Pharisees.

Jesus benefited from the prophets' ways of presenting God's word. He also benefited from the lessons he received from his parents. Mary and Joseph must have been wonderful enablers of their child. We know this had to be so from the way that Jesus taught. Over and over, our Lord redirected people to their own responsibility. He continued to challenge them with phrases like, "What do you think?" "How do you read the law and the prophets?" Surely, there are echoes here of Christ's early training.

Likewise with the parables. Jesus spoke to the people from their own familiar ground. He responded to the emotions and thinking patterns of those he faced. He did not lecture them about God's love or joy. He reminded them of experiences that they had already known and felt. Our Lord used recognizable situations as his raw material for revealing the mysteries of God's kingdom.

All the people could understand how a father could be happy when his prodigal son came home. They could imagine how happy they would be if they found a treasure buried in their field. They had already taken part in the jovial atmosphere of a wedding feast, where grudges are forgotten and guests do all they can to make the day a memorable one.

We have never tired of praising Jesus for his decision to speak in parables: "as we are able to understand them." It would also be well to praise him for the teachers who taught him—those unknown instructors in the synagogue in Nazareth; the prophets of Sacred Scripture who trained him in approachableness and "availability";

and especially Joseph and Mary who were his original and most persuasive guides of the way to grow in wisdom and in grace.

Prayer

In your memory,
think of one or two teachers
(or coaches, or scout leaders, etc.)
who have impressed you deeply
and have helped you grow. . . .

In your imagination,
return to the place where it happened. . . .
Savor the feeling that comes back;
     – how good you felt, just to be with them;
     – how they challenged you to think
        and take responsibility;
     – how they praised you for your achievements;
     – and whatever else it was. . . .

Now let Jesus enter your place.
(It is not necessary to picture him;
just feel his presence. . . .)
Let him explain, as he wants to,
     that his method of teaching was,
     in some respects,
     similar to those good people who taught you. . . .
Give time for this to sink in. . . .

Also, let Jesus tell you
how he learned about guiding others
by the way that Mary and Joseph guided him. . . .
     (Our Lord may want to tell you some specific stories
     that were part of his early years.
     Let him do so, if he wants to. . . .)

Finally, let Jesus instruct you, in practical ways,
how you can be a better guide for others—
     how you can be a good "giver of helpful words". . . .

14

Invited Out

A marriage took place at Cana in Galilee; and the mother of Jesus was there. Now Jesus also was invited to the marriage.

John 2:1-2

Jesus said, "Zacchaeus, hurry and come down, for I must stay in your house today."

Luke 19:5

Jesus addressed this parable to the Pharisees: "The kingdom of heaven is like a king who made a marriage feast for his son. . . . Then he said, 'The marriage feast is ready . . . go to the crossroads and invite to the marriage feast whomever you shall find. . . .'"

Luke 22:1-9

Reflection

St. John had many important things to say about the significance of the "first sign" that Jesus worked at the wedding feast at Cana in Galilee. Probably, it was not his intention to give us a hint about the social life of Mary and her son.

The hint is there, just the same. No one would call Mary a "social butterfly" in the frivolous sense of the term, but there is the feeling that a celebration would not be the same without her presence. The bride and groom at Cana were not Mary's relatives, not even close neighbors. Still, she was invited and added a great deal to the festivities.

It is a lovely way to think of her—gracious, charming, kindly, fun to be with—a large plus of any party.

Jesus must have been proud of her for a long time before that particular wedding feast. It is impossible to think that there were not many more weddings and celebrations in the villages of Galilee. Chances are, Mary was on everybody's list, and they all made special efforts to include her.

Jesus was able to enjoy parties, too. He wasn't left behind. Undoubtedly, there were many more occasions than the one at Cana when "Jesus was also invited."

It must have rubbed off, mother influencing her son in this regard. When we catch up to the three years we know about, the gospels casually mention an impressive number of times when Jesus was asked to dine with the Pharisees. Once Jesus invited himself—to enjoy a good meal with Zacchaeus, the wealthy tax collector.

As a matter of fact, the only real item of contention the Pharisees had was that "Jesus enjoys life too much," dining and celebrating with people of all social strata. Christ's enemies objected, saying that he was overdoing this joy of life. Our Lord complained to them as a child would complain to his sullen playmates: "John the Baptist comes, neither eating nor drinking; and you say, 'He is a fanatic!' The Son of Man comes, *enjoying life*; and you say, 'He is a drunkard and a glutton'" (Matthew 11:18-19. Phillips's translation. My italics.)

This love of life, so well documented in the gospels, is one of the most charming aspects of our Lord's ministry. It was (perhaps it still is) a quality of God's that is very difficult to comprehend. Most people contemporary to Christ had a sense of God that could be described by such words as fierce, haughty, demanding, relentless (in the bad sense), hard to please, quick to find fault, joyless.

The task of the only Son of God was to be born of Mary, grow up slowly, and then—when the time was right—"change the adjectives" that surrounded the sense of who God is. According to Jesus, God is understood by such words as merciful, approachable, kind, easy to trust, easy to be with, relentless (in the sense that he won't give up on us), and quick to start a party as soon as a sheep is found or the prodigal comes home.

So all the social gatherings our Lord attended, all the celebrations he took part in, all the times he dined with people like Zacchaeus and Matthew's tax collectors, all the wedding feasts he went to with his mother . . . all these served as analogies of God. They were the "celebrative material" by which Jesus explained the jovial nature of his Father. Since he spoke of "Abba," God has become a good "daddy" who wants his house of heaven filled with happy guests—guests who are so relaxed they can enjoy his company, and he can enjoy theirs.

Christ's statements about God as the "life of the party" and the "host of a happy homecoming" ran counter to the idea of God as the "diety to be dreaded." For many Christians, even today, Christ's revelation is still counter-culture. Many people still think of God only in terms of demanding the impossible, and disapproving of our simple joys."

God does demand certain things of us, especially love of others, forgiveness of people's wrongs, gratitude for his creative gifts on our behalf. But he demands these things so that we can enjoy the party that he has prepared for us . . . and enjoy the fact that it has already started.

Therefore, it is well for us to have a good time whenever we are invited out. It is not only a good thing in itself. It is also a very good way (the gospels seem to indicate that it is the very best way) to understand the kindness of God and the festive atmosphere of his eternal home. We won't become true citizens of heaven until we can describe ourselves in the same way that the bride and groom of Cana thought about Mary . . . and until we can define ourselves as "enjoyers of life," as did Jesus.

Prayer

Recall the last two or three times when you were invited out
and you had a very good time.
(It may have been a birthday party, anniversary, wedding,
a dinner given in honor of someone, or
whatever. . . .)

Remember how good you felt to be invited. . . .
Feel, once again, the pleasure of "belonging". . . .

Think of how you prepared for it, dressed for it,
looked forward to it. . . .
Then recall the actual event:
 the expected things and the unexpected things. . . .
Finally, remember how you enjoyed the "afterglow"
 as you turned the evening over in your heart. . . .

Now, in your imagination, place yourself in a room
that somehow has mementoes of these occasions. . . .
Leisurely take them all in. . . .

Let Jesus enter.
Let him tell you about how he shares the memory of your joy. . . .
Then let him tell you about the happiness
 that you gave to the host and hostess who invited you.
He will explain how good they felt because you were there. . . .

Finally, let him choose one of the times you were invited out,
 whichever one he wishes,
and by means of the recollected particulars of this joyful experience,
he tells you a new parable about the goodness of his Father. . . .
 (He tells you that God is even better
 than the best host,
 inviting you to the best party in the world. . . .)

15

Hospitality Hints

When the apostles returned [from their first missionary journey] they reported to Jesus all that they had done and taught . . . And Jesus thrilled with joy in the Holy Spirit . . . and praised God.

Luke 10:21-24

Then Jesus said to them, "Come apart into a desert place and rest awhile." For there were many coming and going and they had no leisure even to eat.

Mark 6:30-32

Reflection

The gospels of Mark and Luke report the same incident with different slants. One focuses on Christ's joyful response to the good reports of his disciples' first missionary activity. The other focuses on our Lord's concern that these same disciples rest up and have a nice quiet supper in an out of the way place where they wouldn't be disturbed.

This was a most pleasurable day in our Lord's life. It is good to understand him in both of his roles of graciousness—he was a good guest when he was invited out; he was also a good host when he invited others in.

Being able to enjoy oneself at someone else's party is praiseworthy in itself (as it were, "for the fun of it"). It is also praiseworthy from the standpoint of sound theology, because this enjoyment provides the practical basis by which Jesus can reveal the jovial nature of his Father and the happiness of heaven.

The other aspect is important also. We must be good hosts, too. When we invite people to our home, or in any way welcome friends and strangers with hospitality, we are identifying with God instead of identifying with the invited guests.

It is important to be good at both. Many gospel passages bring out Christ's desire that his friends be able to relax. Often, he summoned his disciples to "come apart" from the tumult and the demands of work. Throughout his ministry, our Lord built in a balance, like breathing: a "going out" to the people who needed him, and a "taking in" of God in deserted places, set apart.

The quiet side of the balance could not be labeled "R & R" (rest & recuperation). There was both a spiritual and communal consideration that made these times more purposeful than simply "weekends off from work." They could be called "P & F": Prayer and Friendship. Jesus invited his disciples to these quiet little parties so they could restore their energy, revivify their prayer life and simply relax in each other's company.

There were many such occasions when Jesus was host during his three-year ministry. (Maybe he was chef, too. At least once that we know of, Jesus had a grilled fish dinner waiting for his apostles John 21:9). Also, there was one time when our Lord supervised a very formal evening. The Last Supper was certainly such an occasion. Jesus was very careful about preparations. He left nothing to chance. He sent Peter and John to a house in Jerusalem: "Tell the owner, 'The master says, "Where is my dining room?"' He will show you a large upper room, furnished with couches, all prepared" (Matthew 26:17; Mark 14:12; Luke 22:7).

Jesus proved to be a thoughtful host and a careful planner for large celebrations—"state occasions," one might say—as well as a congenial host on more informal get-togethers.

The gospels don't even give a hint of Christ's training in this regard. Yet we know there must have been many precedents in his life—many occasions lodged in his memory—to give Jesus such a sure instinct about when to withdraw from his ministry in order to be a good host for a few friends.

How many times did Jesus see Mary in this role? On how many occasions was she hostess at the time of an anniversary . . . or the arranger of a birthday party for a cousin just "come of age"?

And how many thoughtful moments did mother and son share

after the party was over as they cleaned up the house and washed the dishes? Is it not likely that Mary told him how important it is to be gracious and hospitable to others, providing them with a setting where it is easy to celebrate each other's company and have a good time . . . so that all can go back to work with grateful hearts and refreshed spirits?

Perhaps, if we let it happen, Mary will explain these things to us, as she did to her own son.

Prayer

In your memory,
recall two different situations
when you were a good host/hostess at a gathering:

1.   A more formal occasion, like the Passover meal on Holy Thursday.
(This would be a Christmas party, anniversary, wedding feast, etc. . . .)

2.   An informal get-together,
such as the leisurely meals, in quiet places,
where Jesus and his apostles enjoyed each other's company. . . .

Remember and rejoice in the love you gave:
        – the hard work preparing things. . . .
        – the strong desire you had
                that all your guests would be glad they came. . . .
        – and how pleased you were when it all went well. . . .

In your imagination,
go to your kitchen. . . .
pretend it is after the guests have gone.
You are relishing the occasion. . . .

Let Mary and Jesus join you there.
Let our Lord share with you
        the ways of hospitality he learned from his mother. . . .

Then let Mary praise you for your genuine concern for people;
and let her teach you how to be even better
        at being a giver of joy to others
        and a provider of an atmosphere of peace. . . .

16

Silence and Compassion

Seeing the crowd, [Jesus] was moved with compassion for them because they were bewildered and dejected, as sheep without a shepherd.

Matthew 9:35-36; Mark 6:34-41

Again there was a large crowd and they had nothing to eat . . . and Jesus said, "I have compassion on the crowd . . . If I send them away fasting, they will faint on their journey. . . ."

Mark 8:1-9

[Before the feeding of the multitude] a great crowd followed Jesus because they witnessed his signs for the sick. But Jesus went up to the mountain and sat there with his disciples. (An apocryphal gospel adds: "And the disciples sat there with Jesus to learn his silence.")

John 6:1-3

Reflection

All of these texts were necessary to give full attention to those two basic words that point out the "style" of Christ's ministry. Before he healed (or taught or nourished), he "looked upon the people with compassion." That is, before he did things, he felt things. The ever-present motive characterizing all of our Lord's activities was the spirit of compassion.

Jesus was not just a do-gooder. What sets him apart from the more casual kind of benefactor is that he was—and still is—a "suffer-wither." He, as Matthew states in Chapter 13, "took our burdens on himself."

With compassion, he saw that our lives lacked purpose. We were like "sheep without a shepherd." So, moved with compassion, he taught us. The teachings were the real nourishment. Those fish sandwiches that followed were simply the end of a full meal. Barley loaves and fish were the "dessert," so to speak, coming after the main course of Christ's words.

The second time, also with compassion, Jesus saw the crowds (the ones in Galilee, centuries ago, and us today) and knew that we need food for our hearts, not just food for our minds. Without his help, we would not be able to finish our journey. He wants us to make it "all the way home"—to his home, with the Father. So he feeds our hearts lest we faint with discouragement, just as he feeds our minds lest we languish in a state of purposelessness.

Compassion is always the moving quality. Then, deeper in Christ's heart, is another quality that moved compassion. This quality was silence, his quiet, attentive presence before God.

Often he went apart into the mountains or desert places in order to be still. But he could be silent for hours, even with crowds of people milling around. He did so before the first feeding of the multitude. St. John's gospel tells of this prelude to his compassion. "A great crowd followed him . . . but he went up to the mountain. (Presumably the crowd did, too.) Then he sat there with his disciples."

He just sat there, oblivious to the noise of many people clamoring for cures. He was aware only of God. He drew into himself and prayed. A non-canonical gospel hints at the awe-inspiring moment. The disciples, seeing Christ's wordless prayer, gathered around him to "learn his silence."

Apparently, a long time elapsed. Nothing "happened." Jesus just sat there, absorbed in prayer, his disciples beside him.

John then narrates the next step: "When Jesus lifted up his eyes, he saw that a very large crowd had come to him" (John 6:5). The evangelist describes it as though our Lord had been in a deep sleep and woke up to be "surprised" by thousands of people who had been clustering around him ever since early morning. He saw them after his prayer, and had compassion for them.

Therefore, according to the model given us by Jesus, there seem to be two steps prerequisite to the doing of good. We cannot really love until we learn how to be genuinely compassionate. And we cannot have this Christ-like quality until we learn how to be silent before God.

It is not easy to learn silence. It demands training, technique, and discipline of thoughts. We need help to be able to master the difficult art of quiet prayer, waiting upon God's power to move us with compassion.

The first disciples learned it from our Lord. It is realistic to believe that Jesus learned it from his mother. We can presume, of course, that Mary taught her son how to vocalize his prayer. Every good mother does this.

But she did more. She also taught him her silence. We understand, by a connaturality of instinct, that Jesus would sit beside Mary in her stillness and learn how to be quiet . . . just as the disciples learned it from him . . . just as we can learn from them both . . . if we settle down and sit beside them with a courtesy of stillness and the readiness of an attentive heart.

Prayer

Remember the most recent very busy day in your life.
Think of all the rushing around,
all of the hassles
on that fast lane of your hectic schedule. . . .

Leave that day behind you.
Simply let it go, let it be. . . .
As if you were taking a spiritual shower,
wash away the pressure of your busy-ness.
Just for the present moment
    be cleansed of your frustrations and anxieties. . . .

Then, in your imagination,
go to that high hill in Galilee
where Jesus prayed before he fed the multitude. . . .

Do not say anything.
Just be there. . . .
Watch, as the apostles join the Lord:
    they sit down quietly beside him. . . .

Then Mary joins the circle.
Before she folds herself into her stillness,
she looks at you. . . .
By her wordless expression, you understand
    that she prays for your spirit of prayer. . . .
And she invites you to join the circle of the disciples,
    right next to her.
Do so.
Remain there as long as you can. . . .

(This kind of learning will be mysterious,
    different from any other kind of learning.
But you will be taught:
    without words,
    without pictures in your mind,
    without anything that could be described or analyzed—
you will be taught how to be silent before God . . .
and from this silence you will learn true compassion. . . .)

17

Little Children

They brought little children to him, that he might touch them . . .
And Jesus said, "Let the little children come to me and do not hinder
them. . . ." And he put his arms about them and, laying his hands
upon them, he blessed them.

Mark 10:13-16

Jesus said, "If your child asks you for bread, would you give him a
stone? . . ." Well, if you, evil [imperfect] as you are, know how to
give good things . . . much more so will my heavenly Father [give
you bread, not stones]."

Matthew 7:9-11; Luke 11:9-13

Reflection

To guess about Jesus' upbringing, we do not need a vivid imagination. All we need is an uncluttered mind. The words "easy" and
"spontaneous" can be the lever of our understanding. The logic of
"what must have been" goes something like this:

1. There are certain patterns of behavior that keep cropping up in the
gospels, a certain "signature of personality" that reveals the basic
makeup of the inner man. We can tell who Jesus was by the consistent
things he said and did.

2. Also there are patterns discerned in the way that other people
responded to the Lord. This, too, is a give-away of character. If
others—especially children—reacted to Jesus in a consistent manner,
we can tell quite confidently what Jesus must have been like.

3. From this, we can assume that there had to be "precedents of behavior" that accounted for such a constant pattern. (The apple falleth not far from the tree, and the "tree" grew up in Nazareth.) We know almost nothing about the hidden life of Jesus. But we do get some very good hints from the record of his last three years.

Consider the spontaneity of children. They had no trouble climbing up on Christ's lap. All Jesus had to do was call to them and up they rushed, arms outstretched, smiles on their faces, eyes alert for happiness and blessing.

Children are not systematic theologians. They quite judiciously divide grown-ups into two groups: "good guys" (whom they like and trust), and "bad guys (whom they do everything to avoid). Obviously, Jesus was in the first group. They recognized the "happy child" that was still in this grown man. Such spontaneous behavior on their part uncovers the goodness of Christ's own early life. As Jesus blessed the children, he was also blessing his own childhood. And, indirectly, he was blessing Mary and Joseph for giving him that "happy child" he still enjoyed.

So one part of the picture we have of Christ's hidden years can be drawn from noticing how other people responded to him. The other part of the picture comes from listening to our Lord's own words about his childhood.

The words are direct and loaded with good memories. In St. Luke's gospel, Jesus is speaking about prayer. St. Matthew places it in the Sermon on the Mount. On both occasions, Jesus is urging us to trust in the kindness, the nourishing kindness, of God.

Jesus said: "What father (or parent) is there who, when his child asks for bread, will give him a stone? Therefore if you . . . know how to give good things to those who rely on you, how much more will my Father (be a giver of bread, not stones) for you?"

The analogy is clear. God is as good as the best parents caring for their child . . . only God is even better! This is what Jesus said. But we do not know how our Lord puzzled over the problem of how to say it. There was no difficulty about the message itself. The puzzlement was in the explanation.

Perhaps Jesus thought long and hard, searching in his mind for an apt illustration. Perhaps he mused over many similies of trust and goodness, eliminating one after the other as unsuitable. And then he smiled . . . and maybe he said to himself:

"Aha . . . yes . . . that's it! I will tell the people that my Father is like Mary and Joseph, who have nourished me in so many ways. I trusted that my parents would give me bread, not stones. My Father's ways with me are just the same. I must rely on the fact that other parents treat their children kindly, too. And from this experience of routine thoughtfulness given others, I will explain the marvelous goodness of God."

And so it was inserted in the Sermon on the Mount. It is one of the most basic teachings of all. So many parables, and all of Christ's instructions on prayer, develop from this certification of trustworthiness: "God is the giver of bread."

This "God is" statement from our Lord's lips is also a "my parents were" statement about his early years. Bread—in every way that this word is the symbol of nourishment—is what Mary and Joseph gave him. He never got "stones."

If this were not the case, how could he speak so easily about parental kindness? It was the most natural thing for him to think about life this way. It was his life. It was his home experience, long before it became his parable about the Abba-Dear-Father who is in heaven.

Mary and Joseph are in the background of this teaching, just as surely as they were present when Jesus blessed the little children. In both cases, they were blessed as well. They were blessed indirectly.

We, too, can give a blessing to our family: in the same way Jesus did . . . for the very same reasons. Whenever we show kindness to other people (especially to children), we are mirroring the kindness given us when we were young.

Perhaps indirectly is the best approach to learn more about God in the way that Jesus revealed him. Through the insights that come from quiet prayer, we can better understand the kindliness of our Father in heaven. We can trust him more. Also, we can learn to be more grateful for the bread we have received from others . . . and we can learn to be less bitter about the stones.

Prayer

In your imagination,
go to a television studio.
Everything is shut down except for four TV sets.

Mary and Joseph are there, waiting for you.
Greet each other in whatever way seems right. . . .

First, you go over to turn on one TV.
(It is showing a film that you have seen before,
        perhaps too many times before.)
It is a replay of some hurting memories of your childhood:
        – when parents (or family or teachers)
                were insensitive to you;
        – when, somehow, they gave you "stones" instead of "bread."
Do not stay long watching this film. . . .

Let Mary get up and turn it off.
Then she plays some scenes from the second TV:
        – when parents (and others) cared for you;
        – when they helped you, provided for you,
                nourished you in many different ways
                (most of which you have forgotten).
Let Mary remind you of reasons for you to be grateful,
based on past goodness given you when you were growing up. . . .

Now Joseph gets up and turns on TV number three:
this shows scenes from Christ's childhood,
        ordinary incidents when Jesus was given kindly treatment. . . .
(You may not be able to visualize this in prayer;
even so, you can sense it, somehow.
Let the understanding come to you
        in whatever way the Holy Spirit wishes. . . .)

Finally, let Mary arrange a wider screen for
        the fourth TV.
Here you see the scene recorded by the gospels
        where Jesus is calling children to climb on his lap. . . .

See yourself as one of the children . . .

Accept his invitation to come close to him.
Let yourself be warmed by this experience. . . .

When all this is finished
and the room is quiet once again,
let Jesus remind you of people in your own life:
    – family
    – young children and the aged
    – people you meet at work and play
    – and anyone else he wishes to bring up . . .
Let Jesus instruct you
how to be more sensitive to them . . .
And how to be better about giving bread, not stones,
    to all those who need nourishment from you. . . .

18

Time For Everyone

As Jesus was leaving Jericho with his disciples and a very large crowd, a blind man . . . was sitting by the wayside, begging. He began to cry out, "Jesus, Son of David, have mercy on me." Those who were in front angrily tried to silence him. But he cried out all the louder . . . Then Jesus stopped and commanded that he should be called. And they (the same people who had tried to silence him) called the blind man and said to him, "Take courage. Get up. He is calling you."

Mark 10:46-52; Luke 19:35-43; Matthew 20:29-34

Reflection

Only one text was selected for this consideration. If we tried to include all the times Jesus stopped what he was doing in order to give time for someone, we would include most of the gospels. This text was chosen because it was the last recorded miracle before Holy Week. Obviously, the evangelists consider it very important.

The "somebody" Jesus stopped for was a "nobody," a blind beggar. This man was not a noteworthy person, not as the world evaluates such things. In fact, the world (represented by the Pharisees and other people in the crowd) tried to hush him up. They said, in so many words, "Now be quiet! Jesus is a very important person, and he's very busy with matters of consequence . . . so he can't be bothered with trash like you!"

The crowd did everything possible to protect the valuable time of our Lord—presumably, so that Jesus would have more time for the "important people," such as themselves. The reason they pushed that beggar away can probably be explained best by the following "syllogism of snobbery":

Major: God really should be the same as I. And it follows that Jesus, if he is the true revelation of God, should also be the same as I.

Minor: I don't consider myself a snob, of course. But I do feel that my time is too important to bother with insignificant people.

Conclusion: Therefore Jesus should feel the same way. And therefore, that blind beggar has no business interfering with us VIP's!

The process illustrates the reverse side of "bread, not stones" mentioned in the last chapter. The crowd's reaction to the beggar presents a classic case of harshness shown where there should have been kindness. The man was crying out for a healing; instead (by everybody but Jesus), he was shoved back into the gutter.

Human snobbery, so aptly demonstrated by that crowd in Jericho, gives to the world a frightening "negative parable" of God. Jesus said, "My Father is as good as you are, when you are at your best—only he is better." But many people tend to think of God in terms of the silencers of Jericho: "God is like people at their worst (like that crowd with no time for an insignificant nobody), only he is even more cruel and insensitive because he is more powerful and important."

That is to say, many people disregard the teaching of Jesus and still insist that God is the "thrower of stones, not a giver of bread. . . . He is like I am when I act most selfishly and like others when they treat me with harshness or disdain."

The difficulty lies in the very atmosphere we live in. There is a psychological acid rain in our culture that is much more serious than chemical fallout. The instinct of snobbery, to some extent, has infected the jokes we laugh at, the organizations we belong to, the bigotries we breed, the grudges we nurse, and the defenses we build up to save ourselves from inconvenience.

Jesus did his very best to protest this acid rain. By word and by example, he appeals to us to change so that we can learn to understand God in terms of caring nourishment, not in terms of the bigots of Jericho who were too busy to bother with a nobody.

Jesus was never a snob. Over and over again, he made room to welcome everyone, he made time for everyone's request. He insisted—indeed, he "commanded"—that the blind beggar must not be shoved aside.

As was Jesus, so is God the Father. "My Father and I are one," he said. "If you have seen me, you have seen the Father also." From the lips of the son, we know that the Father is just as kindly, just as available as he.

How did this certain instinct about God grow in Christ's human consciousness? We do not know, exactly . . . but we feel that it must have developed at home.

Even though particulars are lost to us, there had to be particulars—Mary stopping her work to listen to a neighbor's problems, because Mary was the only one the neighbor could talk to; Mary rejecting the predjudices of townsfolk by welcoming a "social outcast" into her kitchen; the home of Mary and Joseph, well-known for being a haven for those who felt somehow insignificant.

It had to be this "matrix of experience" that helped Jesus develop into the wonderful welcomer he was. We cannot know this by research. We cannot read about it or "see" it. But a readiness of prayer can make it real to us, once we quiet down enough to let the truth sink in.

Prayer

Remember a hurting experience from your childhood:
> – a time when you were ignored by someone;
> – or you had hoped someone would have had time for you,
> > or be with you,
> > but they were too busy.

And you went to some "brooding place"
and felt sorry for yourself. . . .

Now think of one or two recent put-downs
where much of the same thing happened:
> – friends (you thought they were friends) forgot about you;
> – you were the butt of scorn or sarcasm;
> – a party went on without your being invited;
> – an organization you wanted to join did not want you;
> – some other troublesome memory. . . .

Feel your childhood experience

and your recent experiences
as one cumulative hurt. . . .

Now, in your imagination,
take all the people who have made you feel small and unimportant,
and place them in the crowd outside Jericho. . . .
They are now part of that crowd
    who pushed the blind beggar into the ditch.
Then they push you into the ditch, too. . . .

Do not stay down there!
Do not let them silence you!
Cry out to Jesus, asking for audience. . . .
Let him command them all to stop hurting you.
    Let him invite you to himself. . . .

Tell him about some of the times when you felt miserable. . . .
when it seemed that even God was too busy to bother with you;
when it seemed that everybody in your life
    was bent on making you feel unimportant. . . .

Let him teach you about the Father that he knows. . . .
And let him tell you about Mary—
    the gentle ways she cared for people
    who felt the same way that you feel sometimes. . . .

Let him console you with these thoughts;
then move you with practical advice
    about how to give more time to the "nobodies" in your life. . . .

19

When to Say No

Some people brought Jesus word about the Galileans [massacred] by Pilate . . . And he answered, "Do you think that these were worse sinners than all the other Galileans because they have suffered such things? "I tell you, no. But unless you repent, you will all perish in the same manner. "Or those eighteen people upon whom the tower of Siloe fell and which killed them: do you think they were more guilty than all the other dwellers in Jerusalem? "I tell you, no. But unless you repent, you will all perish in the same manner."

Luke 13:1-5

A man in the crowd said, "Lord, tell my brother to divide his inheritance with me!" [Jesus replied:] "Man, who has appointed me to be your arbitrator?"

Luke 12:13-14

Reflection

There must be balance. From the last chapter, one could get the impression that Jesus always said yes to everybody, that he never said no.

This is one-sided. Jesus did, at times, refuse people who demanded help from him. Sometimes, he refused quite emphatically. We get a distorted picture of our Lord if we think of him as always giving in. Such thinking can lay guilt trips on good people.

It often has. Say you are a good person. You are accosted by certain individuals who demand that you take their side, either by joining their ranks in a protest or cause they are fired up about . . . or taking their side in a family squabble . . . or wasting your time as they rehearse their pet gripes and expect you to agree with them about the unfairness of it all.

These individuals demand your cooperation and they try to make you feel guilty if you refuse. Stated or implied, the procedure goes like this:

1. Jesus never refused anyone.

2. If you are a true Christian, you will want to live like him.

3. Therefore, you cannot refuse my demands and still feel that you are Christ-like!

The argument is wrong because the first statement is not entirely true. Jesus did say no on occasion. It is important to remember this "negative side" of him.

The gospel tells of at least nine times when Jesus refused to attend to the needs of the people because he decided to take time for himself: to rest, to pray, or simply to enjoy a long afternoon with his disciples (Mark 1:35, 1:45, 3:13, 4:35, 6:30, 7:24, 9:29, and 11:11; there are parallel passages in Matthew and Luke).

St. Luke sums it up best (5:16): "Jesus' reputation spread more and more, and great crowds gathered to hear him and to be cured. . . . [but] he often retired to deserted places and prayed." Often! It wasn't every now and then, when he could squeeze it in. It was often.

Such frequency of retirement meant frequency of refusals, because the crowds never let up. A passage in Mark's gospel gives the sense of the bustle of it all: "Wherever Jesus put in an appearance, in villages, in towns, or at crossroads, the crowds scurried about . . . and begged him to let them touch just the tassle of his cloak" (Mark 6:54-55).

Even so, Jesus often retired. Therefore, we cannot say that Jesus was always going about, doing good. He was sometimes "going away, taking rest." It is important to see Christ doing both: agreeing to help and declining to help. In each case, he is teaching us by example.

Our prudence derives from his. Therefore, people should not

call us selfish when we occasionally say no to them. They should not be allowed to manipulate us with their complaints about our never being around when they need us . . . or with their long faces showing resentment over what they consider frivolous pursuits, when what we did was the same thing Jesus often did—we went away to a place apart: to rest, and pray, and play.

Another aspect of resistance is sometimes called for by our Lord's example. There are occasions when we, too, must refuse those who demand that we join their causes. Twice that we know of, people urged Jesus to speak up against social injustice (and presumably start a protest march). The crowd was outraged by a case of polite brutality: Pilate's soldiers massacred twenty people in Galilee. They were also vexed by what was probably political graft: a tower in Jerusalem was constructed so poorly that it toppled down and crushed some bystanders.

Our Lord refused to get worked up against either protest. Certainly, he spoke against social injustice. The Sheep and Goats Parable (Matthew 25:31-46) is the Magna Charta for all people working against exploitation of any kind. But Jesus concentrated on personal change of heart—"Unless you repent"—rather than fan the flames of hatred against certain groups who were already hated by many people.

It would be well to consider both aspects of the ways Jesus said no in order to put yes and no in balance in our own lives. It would be well, also, to consider Christ's training in this regard. He did not acquire such discernment in a vacuum. It is not easy for anyone to know when it is proper to agree to help someone and when it is proper to refuse. Undoubtedly, Jesus was taught how to do so by watching how his parents did it.

We do not know how, or when, Mary and Joseph refused to help people, on occasion. Actually, the popular mentality gives us an altogether one-sided picture of Christ's upbringing. We have the feast day of "Joseph the Worker." By implication, Joseph (and Mary, too?) were always busy. There was nothing but serviceability in their lives—nothing "frivolous" like taking the day off and enjoying a family picnic. If we concentrate only on this task-oriented portrait, we get more of a sense of Ebenezer Scrooge than we do of healthy and happy parents.

It would be good to balance the picture of the Holy Family by celebrating the feast of "Joseph the Player," also. And perhaps we could celebrate another feast: "Mary the Refuser to Say Yes to Everybody's Demands on Her Time."

Ideally, people who have a tendency toward laziness or irresponsibility should focus on:

"Joseph the Worker"
"Mary the Consoler, No Matter How Busy"
"Christ the Sayer of Yes."

While those who tend to wear themselves out with work, getting drained from living up to everybody's expectations, should concentrate more on:

"Joseph the Player"
"Mary the Resolute, When it Came Time for Prayer"
"Christ the Sayer of No."

Of course, the ideal is balance. The best way to achieve this is to pray for it. When we calm down to a quiet mood, we can let God's Spirit give us the wisdom about yes and no . . . and give us the courage to make this wisdom real.

Prayer

In your memory,
recall the last time you had a vacation,
or made a retreat,
that was truly restorative. . . .

Remember how hectic your life had been just before that time. . . .
Remember how the demands on you were so pressing that
    you couldn't do your work very well.
Your capacity to think
    was blocked by trivialities and preoccupations. . . .
Many important people in your life
(friends, family, even God)
were more or less excluded
    because you lacked the energy to pay attention to them. . . .

Then you went off, to the place apart.
You finally slowed down enough to be able to relax. . . .

Remember how good you felt.
Feel it again. . . .
    (Amazing how much more open you were
    to life's purposes and God's possibilities. . . .)

In your imagination,
go back to the place, and the time,
when this happened.
Let Jesus meet you there. . . .
Let him praise you for taking the time off. . . .

He will explain to you
        how important it is to say no to people, sometimes.
He will teach you
in the same way that he taught his first disciples. . . .

Let him also (if he wants to)
tell you about his memories with Mary and Joseph. . . .
Perhaps he will mention certain specific incidents
which he cherishes
when the family went away to enjoy themselves. . . .

Finally, let Jesus repeat for you
some of the advice his mother gave him,
on how to put the right balance in your life:
        – When to say yes to people,
            even though this involves inconvenience for you.
        – And when to say no to them,
            because you, too, need to go off by yourself—
                to rest and pray,
                to restore priorities,
                    and revive a genuine enthusiasm for life. . . .

PART THREE

Mary
With Jesus
During His Active Ministry

20

After You've Said Goodbye

[At the wedding feast at Cana in Galilee] observing that the wine had run short, the mother of Jesus said, "They have no wine." Jesus said to her, "What would you have me do, woman? My hour has not yet come." His mother said to the attendants, "Do whatever he tells you."
. . . This first of his signs Jesus worked at Cana in Galilee; and he manifested his glory and his disciples believed in him. After this, he went down to Capharnaum. . . .

John 2:3-5; 11-12

Reflection

The above selection has omitted many details about the marriage feast at Cana. It was arranged this way to draw attention to an unheralded sorrow of the Blessed Mother, the "marginalization of Mary."

In a way, it was her own fault. She "hurried up" the process that pushed her off into the margin of her son's life. She cared about her friends. She did not want the bride and groom to suffer the embarrassment of being considered stingy or lacking in hospitality.

We do not know what the reason was for the unexpected shortage of wine. Perhaps Jesus was responsible for this. He had been invited to the wedding because he was Mary's son (see Chapter 14). But his disciples had not been invited. They were party crashers, so to speak. At least six disciples (John 1:40-46) attached themselves to Jesus just the day before. Perhaps it was their thirst that quickly drained the supply of wine. If so, it would have given even more reason for Mary to ask her son to do something, maybe to send Peter and Andrew back home to get some of their stock.

Whatever the causes were that led to the situation, the facts were these: gloom was about to ruin the festivities; Mary did not want this to happen; she wanted Jesus to alleviate the crisis.

Our Lord understood her request in terms of an entirely different crisis. If he agreed to his mother's wishes, it would mean that he would begin the time of his active ministry. Once he began his miracles, he would leave home for good and launch into the world as an itinerant preacher . . . a launching that would conclude in Jerusalem where he would suffer the same fate as all the prophets before him.

And so it happened. Really, it was not Mary's "fault" at all. Sooner or later, Jesus would have left home.

The sorrow consisted of a three-year-long "hole in her life" put there by her son's absence. No longer could she call him for supper, or depend on him for heavy chores, or enjoy his company on the porch during the cool evenings. She had to depend on rumors, hints, guesses, second-hand reports (for the most part) telling her about what Jesus was doing in Tyre and Sidon, in the land beyond the Jordan, in the neighborhoods of Corozain and in Jerusalem itself.

Probably he did manage to visit home every now and then. But these vacations only made the goodbyes more poignant. We know there were a few times within the last three years when Mary met Jesus as he was journeying. But these were almost nothing compared to the days and months of being alone in a house that used to be filled with life. Now, her house was a symbol of her "marginalization."

Everyone can understand how Mary must have felt. We all have been "placed in the margin" of somebody else's destiny, one way or another. It is the common experience of parents when their children grow up, leave home, and start the time of their own journey.

It can happen when a friend leaves for another job, or another location . . . after which the friendship simply cannot be the same as it was.

Nobody's fault. It's the way life happens, sometimes. Of course, there can be letters and phone calls. We do have ways of keeping in touch. Now and then, the grown-up children return to pay a visit, or there is a reunion of friends. But it is not the same. Once we are in the margin of somebody's life, we remain in that margin. We must live with it and, as best we can, live with the "hole" left in our life— because the cherished intimacy, which used to be there, is now no more.

This is the kind of sorrow that is too unremarkable to complain about. Yet the silent emptiness of marginal existence does take something away from the life that continues. It is not a jolting sorrow; it is experienced as something like a quiet thud.

Even so, we must continue. We must do what Mary had to do in her emptied-out home at Nazareth. She will help us, if only we have a heart prayerful enough to profit by her guidance.

Prayer

Recall people, special to you
to whom you have had to say goodbye,
such as Mary had to say goodbye to Jesus at Cana. . . .
(Don't try to force yourself to remember all of them.
Let prayer suggest the ones to think about. . . .)

In your imagination,
go to a busy airport. . . .
You are sitting alone,
waiting for your "special friends" to check their baggage
    before they leave for their destinations. . . .

You remember how it happened the first time
—the actual farewell—
You remember, perhaps with some regret,

some of the words you failed to say;
or some of the words you said, and wish you hadn't. . . .

Imagine how you'd like to have those moments back,
in order to do it "right." . . .
    so that the sorrow that follows the leave-taking
    will be good, honest sorrow,
    unspoiled by guilt or remorse. . . .

Let Mary come and sit beside you in the waiting room.
Let her tell you about Cana in Galilee
    and about her loneliness during the years that followed. . . .

Let her suggest the words
and how to express the words,
    as you say goodbye to your loved ones . . .
(This time, it will be more peaceful,
    more gracious than before. . . .)
And let her help you to "let go of them"
as you continue to live in the margin of their lives—
    as Mary, for three long years,
    let go of her son: freely and unselfishly. . . .

21

Handling Snubs

Jesus returned [after the temptations in the desert] in the power of the Spirit into Galilee. . . . He came to Nazareth, where he had been brought up; and, according to his custom, he entered the synagogue. [After he had addressed his townspeople] he said, "No prophet is acceptable in his own country." And all in the synagogue were filled with wrath. And they rose up and put him forth out of the town and led him to the brow of the hill [intending to] throw him down headlong. But he, passing through their midst, went his way. And he went down to Capharnaum.

Luke 4:14-30

Reflection

Traditionally, there are Seven Sorrows of Mary: Simeon's prophecy; the flight into Egypt; the loss of Jesus when he was twelve; meeting Jesus on the way to Calvary; beside the cross, watching Jesus die; receiving the dead body of her son; leaving the area where Jesus was buried.

These are the more remarkable dolors of our Lady. But there were others, no less painful because they were more "ordinary." Two other situations qualify as genuine sorrows: the "marginalization," mentioned in the last chapter, and this one, which could be called the "shunning" of Mary, or her "frigidization."

In a sense, the son had it easy compared to his mother. That encounter between Jesus and all the people in his hometown synagogue was quite dramatic. Then—after the drama—Christ went down to Capharnaum. He continued his ministry in other places. But Mary was stuck with the "at home" consequences of the encounter.

No miracle was performed. The story is one that is often repeated through history (even in John Wayne movies). A great man is resented by the folks back home. The resentment, fed by the fury of group strength, intends to kill the hero who shows them up for their pettiness of spirit. Because of his inner strength, the hero simply eyeballs the cowards down, reduces them to the futility of inaction . . . and abruptly leaves them to brood about their lost battle.

All well and good. Jesus was magnificent, but then he left home. He didn't have to continue to rub shoulders with those small-minded individuals. Mary, however, did remain behind. For about three more years she had to live with the whiplash of this encounter.

It must have been difficult for her. Day in, day out, she co-existed with townspeople who were "shown up" by her son. Such individuals, the world over, are notorious for holding on to grudges. Cowardly souls can be expected to "take it out on others" when their bravado has been unmasked.

Imagine all the cold shoulders, the "frigidization," Mary endured during the months that followed. She would have been snubbed at the well . . . she would have been the target of spiteful words as she entered the marketplace. She used to be the life of every party; now she was singled out to be not invited into anybody's home.

We can understand this feeling. All of us, in one way or another, have been given a cold shoulder by those who used to welcome us warmly. The cause of it could be a relationship like Mary's: we could be friends with somebody who is not liked by a certain group, and they snub us because of our association with the outcast. It could be that a person has just become a widow or widower . . . and the heretofore friendly people suddenly suspect the single person. Cold shoulder again.

Groups also have a way of singling somebody out of their lives. If we become a charismatic, we can be shunned by those not so; if we are not a charismatic, we can be shunned by those who are. If we are smokers or non-smokers, joggers or not, music fans, movie buffs . . . on and on go the possibilities of being left out because of a particular aspect of our lifestyle. These are the milder forms of becoming a social outcast.

There is not much we can do about our frigidizations. If people treat us with disdain (as they treated Mary) because we love somebody they can't stand . . . or if a group finds us unacceptable because of our hobby or manner of prayer or a special interest of some kind . . . there is nothing we can do about it. We cannot change the opinions of what certain individuals consider to be insufferable.

But we cannot let their cold shoulders freeze all the life out of us, either. If Mary was able to continue living, despite the atmosphere of wrath, so must we. Surely, because she "knows the territory," she can help us learn patience. She can teach us about warm hearts—hers and her son's—which can control the thermostats of any number of cold shoulders.

Prayer

In your imagination,
place yourself in an amusement park.
You are all alone. . . .

Take a seat on a conveyer train
that goes through a lifelike wax museum. . . .
It is entitled "Valley of the Snobs."

Slowly be transported through scenes
    that you remember from real life:
Figures of people,
in their most hateful poses,
are treating you as they actually have in the past:
    – whispering about you behind your back;
    – not talking to you any more;
    – treating you disdainfully . . .
Be saddened by these scenes. . . .

Let Jesus come and take his place beside you.
Let him do for you,
What you cannot do for yourself:
    Look them straight in the eye,
    self-controlled,
    undaunted by those petty tyrants. . . .

Then he conducts you to another part of the museum,
the "Palace of Friends" . . . .

Let each wax figure represent a person who has stood by you
     when you were saddened by snubs. . . .
Let Jesus tell you how he, too,
appreciates what your friends have done for you.

The last figure is Mary.
Let this figure come to life. . . .
She joins you, sitting beside her son.
Then she takes your hand and tells you how she managed
     during her three lonely years in Nazareth. . . .

Let her teach you about steadfastness,
about gratitude for the friends you have,
and about how not to get soured on life
          even though there are hateful people
          who have tried their worst to make you do so. . . .

22

True to Your Friends

They came to the house [Jesus and his disciples] and again a crowd gathered so that they could not so much as take their food. But when his own people [from home] had heard of it, they went out to lay hold of him, for they said, "He has gone mad." And his mother and his brethren came, standing outside, and they went to him, calling him. And a crowd was sitting about him and they said to him, "Behold, your mother and your brethren are outside, seeking you." . . . And looking round on those who were sitting about him, he said: ". . . Whoever does the will of God, is my brother and sister and mother. . . ."

Mark 3:20-21; 31-36

Reflection

We know that Jesus was tempted—"tested" is the better word. The gospels of Matthew and Luke describe the first test. It happened in the desert, when Jesus was fasting for forty days. All three temptations urged our Lord to discontinue his project of love. The devil suggested that if Jesus simply loved people he would end up a loser. If he decided to control them, he would win—all the kingdoms of the world would be his.

By means of three different contrasts, Satan pictured a very dismal scene, the prospect of diminishing popularity, unless Jesus changed his gentle ways and took up the tactics of people who use power to get their way. Essentially, the tempter was trying to discourage our Lord. He wanted the prophet of Nazareth to quit his course of loving service.

Perhaps Mary, also, was tempted by the same devil of discouragement. The gospel passages introducing this chapter suggest the battle going on in Mary's soul. With her, it was a temptation tugging at her maternal heart. The mother was being urged to get her son to give up.

"Burnout" was at the bottom of it. The tempter always stands (with one foot) on quite reasonable ground. Jesus was working very hard. Often, he was pressed by the crowds to heal and preach and give of his time and effort in ways that so consumed him that "he could not so much as take his food." At times, he became so weary from it all, he was able to fall asleep on the stern of a boat that was being battered by a storm (Mark 4:35)!

Mary was not part of her son's journeying. For some time, she had been on the margin of his life. She heard secondhand about how hard he was working and how little time he had to rest. She heard many bits of news (no doubt exaggerated by the tellers) that caused her some concern.

Also, her relatives were pushing their arguments in favor of getting Mary to tell her son to call it quits. They would have been Christ's aunts and uncles and cousins on both sides (designated, at that time, as one's "brothers and sisters").

Perhaps they meant well. The best thing one could say about them is that they were family-orientated busybodies who preferred the customary ways of ordinary living and were uncomfortable with the notoriety of Jesus the Wonderworker. They wanted him to settle down and not make waves.

Perhaps they were a part of that "lynch mob" mentioned in Luke's gospel, fourth chapter, who were still bitter about the time when their cousin "walked through their midst and went his way."

Whatever the cause, or combination of causes, they were doing their best to get Mary to join them in their contention that Jesus was on the verge of burnout, that he had over-extended himself.

She did accompany the contingent made up of her kinsfolk from Nazareth. Mark's gospel does mention that Mary was present when the family protested that Jesus was working too hard, that he had "gone mad." But what was Mary doing there? What were her thoughts?

It cannot be imagined that, even tacitly, she was lodging a protest against her son's activities. Such a statement would be tantamount to pulling up the white flag of surrender. Mary did not give in to discouragement or anxiety. Probably, she accompanied her family because she wanted to see how her son was going to handle the show-down. She wanted to see this for herself, not get it by heresay after it had been filtered down by her family's prejudices.

She did. She saw Jesus refusing to be ruled by other people's demands, or worldly "prudence." Notwithstanding the critics of his own family circle, the will of God was the only motivating force in his life. And those who determined to live like him were the only "family" he cared about . . . they were brother and sister and mother to him.

Perhaps Jesus glanced at Mary when he said those words. A glance would have been all that she needed. She was mother to Christ in a new way, now. Her silent support of his cause—at the very time when others were refusing to support him—earned her a new place, a new "family membership," in the kingdom started by her son.

Mary was assured. She went back home relieved. The devil of discouragement could no longer tempt her. She now would stand apart from her family and their critical complaints.

Because of Mary's steadfastness during that celebrated show-down, she can be a great help when we are tempted in the same way. We too, at times, are faced with what could be called a "crisis of loyalty." We hear reports about somebody we love. The reports are critical. Other friends (and members of our family) keep bringing up what is wrong about the individual . . . how she or he is wasting too much time, is working too hard, is becoming indifferent to old ties . . . things like that.

Critics can be powerful through their intimidation. We need strong love to stay true to our friend under such circumstances. We need some way to be our own person, not swayed by the negative accounts of tale-bearers.

Mary can help us in this. She can be for us what she was for Jesus: a "sister and mother" for us . . . and a loyal friend, teaching us about loyalty toward those we love.

Prayer

In your imagination,
go to a crowded living room. . . .

The air is electric with complaints and negative remarks. . . .
In the room are a few family members
and the most critical people that you know.
They are in the worst of moods:
    catty,
    abusive in their manner of speaking,
    bringing up all that is objectionable about a friend of yours. . . .
Stay there, as long as you can stand it. . . .
Then leave them abruptly (without excusing yourself).
Walk slowly toward the kitchen
and close the door. . . .

(As you do this,
realize how they had almost persuaded you. . . .
They threatened your peace;
they raised your anxiety level. . . .
You almost went over to their side
    because some of their reasoning was sound—
    some of it—
    and they seemed so terribly sure of themselves. . . .)

Sit down at the kitchen table;
breathe a sigh of relief, that you weren't taken in. . . .
Let Mary join you.
She pours you, and herself, a cup of tea. . . .
Over the kitchen table
she tells you about her encounters with her critics. . . .

Ask her for suggestions
about what to do in your situation. . . .
Insights will come
    with the stillness of prayer
    and the felt compassion of Mary. . . .

Perhaps you will be told, in practical ways,
how to be more deserving of Christ's praise. . . .
So that he will say to you
what he said to Mary:
    "They who do the will of God
    are brother and sister and mother to me."

23

Not Using People

Now it came to pass, as he was saying these things, that a certain woman from the crowd lifted up her voice and said to him, "Blessed is the womb that bore you and the breasts that nursed you!" But he said, "Rather, blessed are they who hear the word of God and keep it."

Luke 11:27-28

Reflection

After Cana, whenever Mary is mentioned, or alluded to, it is always in terms of a larger family than before—a family her son was giving birth to. Therefore favoritism was foreign to Christ's ministry.

As we saw in the last chapter, Mary was with her relatives who tried to get Jesus to slow down. Our Lord refused to be influenced by them. He "switched family ties," so to speak. Jesus assumed the role of patriarch, and adopted his mother into his new association—with "those who do the will of my Father in heaven."

Here, on another occasion, a woman from the crowd expressed herself in a most natural way. Her maternal sensitivities distracted her. She started to think about how happy must be the mother who brought this marvelous preacher into the world. Undoubtedly, she was also thinking about her joy, if she were the one who could claim kinship with such a remarkable man. She gave utterance to her thought, shouting over the words of Christ: "How happy the womb that bore you and the breasts you sucked!"

The woman meant well . . . but she did get Jesus off the track by this interruption. She was missing the point of all the important teachings Jesus had uttered before she spoke out. She was thinking of the mother's good fortune to enjoy "bragging rights" about her son's popularity. (Perhaps, she was also thinking about the special honors Mary would have, once Jesus reached his ultimate political destiny.)

Our Lord straightened out this misconception. Mary is blessed, indeed, not because of her physical association with him, not because of past ties, but because of her spiritual affiliation. She heard the word of God and kept it.

Very likely, the woman in the crowd is representative of all the people who made comments of this kind. How frequently would Mary have been told about her good fortune? Perhaps neighbors swelled the chorus of her acclaim. Perhaps they pointed out Mary's new-found prestige, based on her son's ability to enthrall the multitudes. Perhaps, also, they urged her to "use her influence," now that he was such a famous man.

Maybe there were people who suggested she take advantage of her situation—perhaps by procuring things she could not afford before; perhaps by "getting back" at her neighbors in Nazareth who were still snubbing her.

It is not uncommon for a person to be given such "practical advice." A man becomes a politician; some members of the family will try to use this "clout" for personal gain. A woman wins the state lottery; people come out of the woodwork to suggest how the money should be spent. When a person is given a position of power (in the form of prestige, money, or influence), there will be some individuals who can think only in terms of how this power can further their selfish purposes.

Mary, of course, was not even tempted by this kind of badgering. Jesus said as much when he responded to the woman in the crowd. If Mary had used clout, based on her family connections, she would have been selfish and an obstacle to her son's ministry. She was neither. She did not follow anybody's persuasion that she use her "association with the powerful" for feathering her own nest.

Jesus praised his mother at the same time that he rebuked the woman who interrupted him. It was a mild rebuke (after all, the woman meant well; she was just superficial and easily distracted). Jesus told her to concentrate more on spiritual responsibility, rather than rest on privilege.

But within this mild rebuke, our Lord was severely restraining a certain tendency we all have, a particular aspect of selfishness and/or vanity that seeks to make personal gain out of someone else's position. This kind of thing crops up in a variety of ways:

- The tendency to be a "name dropper"
  in order to feel important;
- The urge to "get my share" in a windfall
  suddenly enjoyed by friend or family:
- The prompting to get lazy when an associate
  achieves success in such a way that we could
  coast along with it, if we wanted to.

There are always advisors who will tell us that the option of personal advantage is the one that we should take.

Mary's good influence will be most helpful when we are tempted to give in to such forms of "shirttail selfishness." Other friends will help also—the friends who are truly Christ-like. And Mary will help us, most of all.

Prayer

In your imagination,
go to a public library.
Enter a cubicle where you put on a headset
    and listen to records, all by yourself. . . .
First, put on a record that has duplicated words of advice
coming from the most selfish persons that you know.
Listen to all their comments:
- how you should use your family connections
    for your own personal advantage;
- how you should demand that old friends,
    whom you once did favors for,
    should now pay you back . . . "because they owe you";
- how you should think more of your financial security
    and use people
    in order to get ahead in the world. . . .

Listen to these statements as long as you can stand it. . . .

Then turn off that record.
Or, if you find that you cannot do so,

let Mary turn it off for you. . . .
(She has quietly entered the booth and sits beside you. . . .)

Mary puts on another record.
Now, listen to good advice, from your real friends:
  – about honest pleasure you can take
      in your family's achievements;
  – about developing the best that is in you,
      whether you "get the breaks" or not;
  – about doing the will of God,
      without taking advantage of others in any way. . . .

Finally, let Mary take off your earphones
and just talk to you, person to person.
She may relate how she had to resist advice
    from the power-orientated people in her life.
Also, she may share with you the joy she felt
when she learned, from one of the disciples,
that, one day, in the middle of his preaching,
Jesus blessed his mother for the right reasons:
    because she had heard the word of God and kept it. . . .

You will learn from her story
how to be blessed by Jesus
      in the same way,
      for the same reason,
      thanks to the very same affiliation. . . .

24

Perseverance in Prayer

Jesus was teaching . . . and behold, there was a woman who for eighteen years had had a sickness caused by a spirit; and she was bent over and utterly unable to look upwards. When Jesus saw her, he called her to him and said to her, "Woman you are delivered from your infirmity . . ." And the Lord said [to the ruler of the synagogue]: "This woman, daughter of Abraham as she is, whom Satan has held bound for eighteen years, ought she not be loosed from this bond on the Sabbath?"

Luke 13:10-16

Reflection

Mary is not mentioned in Jesus' encounter with a woman who had been bent over for a long time. But it would seem that Mary was prominently "behind the scenes" just the same.

The reason for suggesting this is provided by our Lord's knowledge of the length of the woman's malady. Eighteen years is a different measure of duration than "a long time." It would seem that Jesus had been counting the years. He knew it exactly.

The woman lived in Herod's country (see Luke 13:31). Chances are, she was well known by the family of Nazareth. If Jesus was thirty-two years old at the time of the incident, he would have been fourteen years old when the woman was first afflicted, "bent over double by the evil spirit."

Perhaps Mary introduced the woman to her teenage son:

"Jesus, I want you to meet my friend, ———." Then they had a nice visit . . . Jesus kneeling on one knee so that he could talk with her and see her face at the same time . . . Jesus marveling at her faith, despite the terrible disability.

Doubtless, our Lord needed no prodding to pray for her. From that time on, the Holy Family continued to ask God for her healing. If they prayed for her every night for eighteen years, it would have been 6,570 times that their prayers went unanswered! Many people have given up on God because of the "frustrations of sameness" that lasted less than this.

Yet Mary persevered—Jesus too—even though it seemed that God was deaf to their petitions. Then it happened, one Sabbath, in a quietly spectacular way. At last, their prayers were answered.

Probably this is why our Lord was especially emotional as he rebuked the ruler of the synagogue. On other such occasions, when he healed on the Sabbath, Jesus focused attention on God's mercy and on his own power as "Lord of the Sabbath." Here, in this one case, the focus was on the woman—a daughter of Abraham—who "ought to be healed of her infirmity" . . . an infirmity that lasted all that specific number of years.

Mary was somewhere not far off. Perhaps she was actually in the crowd that day. Whether or not, she undoubtedly heard about it soon after. There had to be some people who knew about the bond of friendship between Mary and the woman. News would have traveled fast, this kind of news. (Jesus would have made sure that it did.)

What expressions of gratitude must have filled Mary's heart. She would have spontaneously expressed her thanks: to God, for the wonderful healing; to her son, for the beautiful way in which he proved to be more powerful than evil spirits; for the woman, because she was able to hold her head up high; and for herself, because she persevered, believing in God's goodness despite unanswered prayers.

Mary can be the anchor of our hope when we are praying for someone in a way similar to the eighteen years of "nothing" through which mother and son pleaded for the healing of their friend. It is hard to keep hope alive under such circumstances. But without this hope, faith can die. Then prayer surrenders. Hope is the virtue that must be nurtured. Healing is possible, always possible, in the mercy of God . . . according to his will.

Confidence in this "possible with God" is possible to us. It is made even more so if we ask Mary to help us.

Prayer

In your imagination,
go to a church that has good memories for you. . . .

Remember the various moods you have been in
when you have prayed for someone
over a long period of time (maybe even eighteen years)
    and nothing has happened. . . .

The person is still in the same fix:
    – still afflicted by physical evils
    – still strained by financial worries
    – still controlled by alcoholism, drug addiction,
        or some other condition that says "no" to life. . . .
Recall your different feelings as you prayed to God:
    – angry at him, at times;
    – puzzled by his apparent obstinacy to your prayers;
    – questioning his very existence, maybe;
    – even threatening to abandon your faith in him. . . .

Let Mary come and kneel beside you.
You both pray silently for a while. . . .
Then she invites you to a quiet room, over to the side.
It is the "room of reconciliation."

After you make yourselves comfortable,
Mary tells you of all the moods she had
as she prayed, for so long, for her friend bent over double. . . .
    (Perhaps she will reveal to you
    the days when she, too, was discouraged. . . .
    She may tell you
    how she continued to hope for healing
        even though there were no results. . . .)

Let Mary console you with the idea
that all of the different kinds of prayer are valid—
even the prayer that sometimes gets angry at God. . . .

And let her help you to be patient,
during your moods of frustration and futility,
    so that you may continue to hope,
    beyond hope,
    that Jesus will discover the day that is the right day
    to heal the person who is your friend,
    and his. . . .

25

God's Upbeat Messages

Jesus said, "What woman, having ten coins, if she loses one, does not light a lamp and sweep the house and search carefully until she finds it? And when she has found it, she calls together her friends and neighbors, saying, 'Rejoice with me, for I have found the coin that I had lost.' Even so, I say to you, there will be more joy among the angels of God over one sinner who repents."

Luke 15:8-10

Reflection

This parable is usually referred to as the "Lost Coin." It is misnamed. According to the emphasis that Jesus gives the story, it should be called the "Found Coin."

It is sandwiched between two other misnamed parables: "The Lost Sheep" and "The Prodigal Son." All three titles, by a kind of human instinct for gravitating toward the dismal side of things, pay attention to what is wrong (or lost, or saddening, or causing misery) rather than on what is joy-inducing.

That was one of the faults of the Pharisees. St. Luke alludes to this very fault when he introduced this set of parables. He locates the scene of Christ's triple revelation of his Father against the background of a bunch of killjoys. A group of Pharisees were "murmuring" against Jesus for having such a good time in the company of unacceptable "tax collectors and sinners." It was to contrast this pharisaical mood of sullenness that we have three of the most beautiful stories of the life-celebrating tenderness of God.

Jesus often rebuked self-righteousness and its accompanying spirit that so complacently decides who is, and who is not, worthwhile. He always defended his right to befriend anyone who would come to him with an open mind and a humble heart.

On this particular day, he did it by means of three parables. One would have been enough. Even two would have been ample for putting his point across. Yet he chose three. The heroes of the first and last story are both males, obvious analogies of the Father. Joy was the telling emotion manifested by the shepherd who found his sheep and the merciful father who got his errant son back safe.

But something seemed to move Jesus to tell another story and put it between the two male figures. This was a story of a woman. She is the one who served as the analogy of a joyful God. She was the hostess of an impromptu party, where friends and neighbors were invited to celebrate because she found a valuable coin.

The coin had to be more significant than a piece of pocket change. No ordinary turn of good luck is cause enough to knock on neighbors' doors, urging them to attend a party that's just beginning. Probably, the coin was part of the gift that Joseph gave Mary at their wedding. (Such a custom still exists among some ethnic groups—a bridegroom gives his bride a set of coins to indicate his trust in her as wife and their "mutual responsibility" as a married couple. It seems that this custom prevailed in Galilee, twenty centuries ago. If so, it would have been an integral part of the wedding between man and wife.)

When the lost coin is understood as a part of the covenant of marriage, it becomes something like a wedding ring. Therefore, it is much more valuable than a drachma or a fifty-cent piece. It also becomes a much more beautiful illustration of God's all-inclusive love. Every human being is a part of God's covenant. When any part has been lost, God becomes a "wife" who "searches diligently" to induce the sinner to return.

It may have been the sight of Mary in the audience that sparked this parable. Maybe there was a twinkle in Christ's eyes, and a smile on his face, as he began. Maybe Mary responded with a smile of her own. She already knew what Jesus was going to say.

Perhaps it was their "secret" as well as his teaching . . . because they both remembered, years ago, one afternoon, when the real incident had taken place exactly in the way that Jesus told it. It was one of Mary's coins that was mislaid . . . and they both searched diligently . . . and when it was found, mother sent son out to invite friends and neighbors to celebrate with her.

This may have been the actual background of the parable. We won't know, for certain, until we get to heaven. But it is good, before we get there, to think of Mary's joy in providing the "raw material" for her son's illustration of God's joy. If we understand that Mary helped Jesus to "find good stories to tell," we can begin to discover upbeat incidents in our own life—happy turns of events and unexpected "findings of what we had lost" that can be the material by which Jesus can speak to us about his Father's happiness.

Either way—by meditating on the stories of the gospel or reflecting on the stories of our own life—we must be sensitive to the "upbeat nature" of these events. We must concentrate on the good feelings that came after the adventure, rather than dwell on the personal discomfort that accompanied the search.

Otherwise, we do not comprehend Christ's teaching. We do him a disservice when we place emphasis on the anxiety that was paramount during the "lost" sequence—searching the mountains and countryside for the sheep, the long hours of poking through corners before the coin was found, the longer months of waiting until the prodigal son returned.

God does not punish sinners with a rehearsal of "What a terrible ordeal I went through . . . And how I worried . . . All the time you were gone!" God is not as we are, usually emphasizing what was wrong (and how I suffered) before the happy ending came about.

God, as revealed by Christ, concentrates on what went right, not what was wrong. This was Jesus' method in all his parables about God's mercy. He was "upbeat"; he wants us to be upbeat also. He tells us to be instructed by his method of telling stories, as well as by the message that his stories convey. A necessary part of his method is *not* to be led by our inclination to nag others about their faults or be righteously self-sacrificing about our hours of anxiety.

Mary can guide us into a re-interpretation of our own adventures. She can help us with the lesson plan of Christ.

Prayer

In your imagination,
go to the center of a small town you never saw before. . . .

Jesus is on the steps of the bandstand
talking to a crowd of people in the park. . . .
He is trying to think up some good stories
    that will serve as illustrations
    of how joyful his Father is
    when a sinner returns to be loved by him. . . .

He turns to you,
looking into your face,
scanning your heart.
    Perhaps he can discover a good story from you. . . .

But you don't have any for him:
    – Recall the last time you lost something valuable.
        Concentrate on the unhappiness you had
        as you were searching;
        and how much time and trouble you wasted until you
        found it. . . .

    – Recall, also, the last time you "lost" a friend.
        Revivify your hurt—
        how painful it was to wait for him or her to telephone,
        to apologize,
        to somehow explain why you were abandoned so
        abruptly. . . .

Rehearse the ways you nursed your grievance
for all the anxious moments you went through. . . .

Jesus reads these recollections of miseries
and cannot find a story to fit what he wants to say about God.
He turns to others in the crowd,
    trying to read some memory of happiness in their hearts. . . .

While he is looking elsewhere,
let Mary join you. . . .
Let her gently turn your stories over
    so that you concentrate on the gladness
    and the relief you felt
    when you:
        – Found the precious article you had lost. . . .
        – Reunited with your friend who had given up on you. . . .

Let Mary suggest even more reasons for your joy
on these occasions. . . .

Then Jesus returns to you.
He looks into your face once again. . . .
Now he recognizes those good stories in your memory. . . .

He smiles,
nods to you in appreciation,
and then he teaches the people about God's true nature,
    based on the joy that he has found in you. . . .

26

Cloaks We Cling To

They brought the colt to Jesus and, throwing their cloaks over the
colt, they set Jesus on it. And as he went, they kept spreading their
cloaks upon the road.

Luke 19:35-36

They brought the colt to Jesus and threw their cloaks over it and he sat
upon it. And many spread their cloaks upon the road, while others
were cutting branches from the trees and strewing them on the road.

Mark 11:7-8

Reflection

Palm Sunday seems to be misnamed. The branches cut down from
the trees are mentioned as quite secondary to cloaks. Indeed, St.
Luke's gospel relates that nothing but cloaks were laid down on the
ground to give Jesus a kind of "red carpet treatment" as he trium-
phantly entered the Holy City.

By gospel implication, this day should be called "Cloak Sunday," or, better yet, "Trust in Christ as My Security Sunday."
Although the second suggestion is too clumsy to be a title, the idea
contained in it is gospel truth . . . and gospel teaching.

A person's cloak, at that time and place, was a poncho of
multiple purposes. It was a cover against the storms by day. It was a
blanket against the cold by night. The garment was a symbol of
personal security. Over and over, the Bible warns wealthy people not
to keep a man's clothing overnight, even if it is a mortgage on a loan:

If you take your neighbor's cloak as a pledge, you shall return it to him before sunset. For his cloak is his; it is the only covering he has for his body. What else has he to sleep in? (Exodus 22:23-24)

Jesus himself measured the greatest demand of charity in terms of letting go of one's most prized possession in order to help another: "If one takes your tunic, give him your cloak as well" (Matthew 5:42; Luke 6:29).

Symbols that would be equivalent to cloaks in our world would be our bank account, our food stored up for tomorrow, our stocks and bonds accumulating interest, our insurance policies—indeed, all the things that permit us to be somewhat sure of ourselves . . . holding on to a sense of protection from possible hardships in the future.

On Palm/Cloak Sunday, the people in the crowd threw away their most treasured security as an act of reverence to Jesus, whom they proclaimed as their Christ and Lord. Such a gesture was a sign that they put their trust in him, not in things.

For most of that large throng, the throwing of their cloaks turned out to be an empty gesture. They proved that they did not trust Jesus all that much. They soon left him to face the Sanhedrin alone . . . and they were conspicuous by their absence when only a few stood by the cross.

But there was a "handful" of faithful ones who really meant it. They really did divest themselves of personal security, putting their faith totally in Christ's hands. Mary was one of them. Surely she was part of the Hosanna Parade that morning. We know that this triumphal entry had been planned ahead of time (Matthew 21; Mark 11; Luke 19). There is no reason to suppose she wasn't there, repeating, now in a new way, the fiat of faith she gave God at the Annunciation . . . fulfilling the condition stated by her son some months before: "Blessed are they who hear the word of God and keep it."

Hosanna Sunday ushers in all the events of Holy Week. We do this day a disservice by focusing on palms. Nothing special about them. Anybody can cut down a few branches. The effortless activity of breaking off some twigs is no way to begin our prayerful reflection on the huge drama of Holy Week. Much more is taught by the personal garment strewn before Christ's path than by the accessible branches of nearby palm trees.

The message of the cloaks is a challenge of trust in Christ. It is a very serious call to become uncomfortably insecure. The week begins with a clear-cut challenge of choice: Do we really believe in Jesus, or are we compulsive about material comfort? Either Christ is the vital source of our security, or the protective assurances provided by our possessions are the source of our security. Fundamentally, it is God or Mammon—Christ, or the "cloaks" we cling to.

Jesus will see to it that our heavenly Father, "knowing all our needs," will provide us with sustenance for survival (Matthew 6; Luke 12). But we must first of all forego all claims to personal control. This is the message of Cloak Sunday. It isn't easy. Jesus did not promise that it would be easy. But it can be done. Mary did it, and so did the disciples, after Pentecost.

The mother of Christ will engender in us the courage necessary to be free enough to trust God, despite our natural reluctance to let go.

Prayer

In your imagination,
walk, all alone, on a summer afternoon,
beside a busy four-lane highway. . . .

You are distressed by the noise, the dust,
    and the fumes of fast-moving vehicles. . . .
Discomfort is doubled by the heavy load you carry.
(They are a bother, but they seem necessary for your security:
    – a luggage bag loaded with much more than you really need;
    – a thick sweater, in case the weather changes;
    – over the sweater, a yellow windbreaker,
        so that cars and trucks will notice you as they zoom
        by. . . .)

Feel the burden of all this,
and the heat of your skin,
    because you want to be "safe". . . .

Now turn aside from the highway;
walk a few hundred yards down a narrow road
    lined with shade trees. . . .

Let Jesus and Mary meet you at a turn in the road. . . .
Let them convince you to free yourself from the luggage
    and the heavy garments on your back. . . .
Jesus gives you a light traveling bag,
    containing only the essentials. . . .
Let him tell you, in his own way, what they are:
    and why you have these things
    and not other things. . . .

Let Mary remove the raincoat and heavy sweater for you.
She gives you a cotton shirt instead. . . .
Feel the difference in the day now;
    feel how free you are. . . .

Let Mary warn you about the dangers
    of worrying so much:
    – worrying about what might happen to you
        financially or physically
        (as symbolized by the luggage and heavy sweater);
    – worrying about other people—
        whether or not others will notice you, or hurt you
        (as symbolized by the yellow windbreaker)

Let her guide you to Jesus. That is her role.
Let her teach you to trust him more. . . .
(She may have some specific things to say to you
about trust.
Give her your time and attentiveness, as long as you can. . . .)

27

Patience, Despite Evil

Behold, one of those who were with Jesus, reached out his hand, drew
his sword, and struck the servant of the high priest, cutting off his ear.
Then Jesus said to him, "Put back the sword into its place; for all those
who take the sword will perish by the sword. Or do you suppose that I
cannot entreat my Father and he will, even now, furnish me with
more than twelve legions of angels? How then are the Scriptures to be
fulfilled, that thus it must take place."

Matthew 26:51-54

Reflection

It is most unlikely that Mary was in the crowd when a squad of
soldiers, led by Judas, took Christ prisoner early in the morning of
Good Friday. Mary heard about these happenings secondhand.
Probably she was with the women waiting for the frightened apostles
to join them in the upper room. This room would serve as the
headquarters for the first church. Probably she was there.

We can only guess about how she felt. Our guess will be a good
one if we trace her thoughts with recollections of ourselves when we
were in similar circumstances. One way or another, we all have been
beset by what could be called "futile sadness"—that terrible pain we
had when someone we love was suffering and we could not do one
thing about it.

All we could do was stay where we were . . . and grieve.
Something tragic happened to a loved one: a terrible accident, a

paralyzing injustice, a circumstance of war or personal hatred that was brutalizing. . . . These would be afflictions somewhat like Christ's suffering on Good Friday. The experience of evil happened to the loved one, and we could not help. We could not change anything. We couldn't even say anything. Our sadness itself was futile. All we could do was feel it.

So it must have been with Mary. We can understand her sorrow from similar situations in our lives. Therefore, it is good for us to reflect on how she managed when she faced the apparent "upper hand of evil." She can help us when we face it in our lives.

Nothing in the gospel indicates that Mary was giving vent to anger at the world (or at God) because of the unfairness of it all. Jesus was being scourged—the sport of soldiers. Then he was mocked with a crown of thorns. Mary heard reports about how the morning went. As the cruelties were disclosed, her face probably turned pale, her breath was short, her body became limp. She was hurting, deeply hurting, inside. But she did not collapse, or weep uncontrollably, or blurt out angry phrases that began with "Why . . . !" She simply hurt, and continued to live.

There was no way to soften her sorrow. She had no magic turn of thought that could erase her compassion for her son's pain and humiliation. But even as she grieved, she had a faith that hung on to something noble. There was a dignity about that day that gave her patient calm. With this, she could face all the other indignities. She saw a significance—even a value—in her son's passion.

Jesus provided the dignity for her. It was contained in the last words he said to Simon Peter. When Peter drew his sword and cut off the ear of one of the soldiers, Jesus bent down, picked up the ear, put it back in place, and healed the man instantly. Then he told his disciples not to use force of any kind. And then he reasoned with them. He reminded them that he didn't need their help. If he wanted to use force, he had armies of angels he could muster on a moment's notice. But love was the only way he would relate to people. Love would prove itself to be more powerful than force. So he would suffer the scourging—and even death itself—if the free will of evil people determined to do this to him. But love would win in the end.

Love was significant on the day that had such horrors in it. The healing of the soldier's ear was the hint of hope that gave meaning to all the virulence of everything else that went on that day. Evil did seem to prevail. But love would be victorious, ultimately. Why else would Jesus decide to heal the soldier and to muzzle his disciples' swords? He could have called on mobilized troups of angels. He chose love, instead.

So Mary was content. This is not to say that she was relieved. She still suffered. But she also shared with her son the conviction of love's supremacy. She was with Jesus in sensing the absolute worth of being true to oneself, no matter how this truth would be taunted with blaspheming mockery.

Mary will give us a share in the same conviction, if we ask her to. She will not take away our grief. She cannot do this any more than she could take away her own, or her son's.

But she will balance our sorrow with a stance of courage in the face of all misfortune. No one—not angels, not even Christ himself—can force people to turn from evil and do good. But no evil should force us to forswear the truth that is in ourselves, or the good we still can do.

There is a turning point to tragedy, a choice that we can control, even though we have no control over the tragic events themselves. The choice is this: are we to let the events turn us to bitterness or despondency? Or are we to turn to the hint of hope Jesus offers us by his healing of the soldier's ear?

Mary decided well. She kept firm hold on her hope. She will help us hold on, too . . . when a tragedy challenges us in somewhat the same way.

Prayer

In your imagination,
sit by yourself, in a dark room.

You have just finished watching the evening news on TV.
You are now in silence. . . .
With your memory to help you,
recall an instance of social injustice
    that has particularly moved you
    as you watched the world news. . . .

Suppose you are the mother or father
of one of those people suffering so much. . . .

Feel the sadness of the situation—the futile sadness—
as you grieve with them
and are unable to help in any way. . . .

Let this sadness increase in you
as you link your compassion for groups of people
with some personal situation of your own:
    – concerning someone you love;
    – or someone you know as a friend
        who has suffered from serious injustice. . . .
You are deeply hurt
by the apparent upper hand of wicked people . . .
and you are powerless to change the situation. . . .

But feel, at the same time,
your pride in the person that you love.
Like Jesus, the person did not give in to evil,
    did not prove traitor to principles,
    did not fight wrong with another wrong. . . .

Now let Mary enter your room
and sit beside you in the darkness. . . .
Let her share with you some of the thoughts she had
about the "upper hand of evil"
    on that Good Friday morning
    after she learned about her son's capture. . . .
And let her tell you about how proud she was
    of Christ's composure
    when he healed the soldier's ear
    and told Peter to put back the sword. . . .

Then let her invest you with quiet courage,
    even as you are frustrated
    by so much evil in the world. . . .
She will give you her spirit of patience and perseverance
    so that you may continue
    to share Christ's ultimate supremacy of love. . . .

28

How to Stand
When You Can't Stand It

Standing by the cross of Jesus [was] his mother. . . .

John 19:25

Reflection

There is a phrase that everyone has used, in one way or another: "I can't stand it! I just can't stand any more!" Mary's position beside the cross of Christ embodies such a situation.

Before we go into the more devastating aspects of desolation, it would be well to make distinctions. Not every suffering is so intolerable that we are reduced to absolute inaction. Sometimes, when we say we can't stand it, the proper remedy is not to stand there, but to move:

- Take a walk, until things settle down.

- See a doctor or counselor who will find ways to remove the causes of distress.

- Give distance to the turmoil by taking a vacation, or taking up a hobby that will be therapeutic.

That is, sometimes, when we are faced with the "intolerable," we can find an alternative to help us move away from it.

Sometimes. But there are other times when creative remedies will not be able to do the job. These are the situations that really qualify as ultimate distress. We are "at the end of our rope." We have asked to be patient for too long. The saddening events have pushed us so far that we feel unable to contain ourselves. We want to give vent to irrational outrage or inconsolable despair, to declare our incapacity to cope: We "just . . . can't . . . stand . . . it!"

It is during such insufferable traumas that Mary's stance at the foot of the cross can be a healing meditation. After all, has there ever been anyone who has been treated worse than Mary? Doesn't her suffering on Good Friday afternoon qualify as the most intolerable of situations?

1. Her son was dying at such a young age. Thirty-three is young. There was so much more healing and teaching he could have done; so much more loosening of the bonds of Satan, freeing people from their chains of despondency.

2. Mother as well as son were suffering from gross injustice. Neither had done anyone any harm. On the contrary, multitudes were healed and fed and given hope again. When Jesus preached to the people, they all marveled at his teaching. Yet their leaders, "out of envy" (Mark 15:10), devised a trumped-up charge and forced his execution.

3. On top of this were:
– Insults. The soldier's slap on the face, the cohort's scourging, Pilate's pretension of investigation, Herod's gesture of contempt. All insults.
– Mockery. The crown of thorns and the royal robes! The way mercenaries taunted the very things that made Jesus who he was. He claimed to be the source of wisdom, the guide to God, the king and leader of his people. He was mocked for being just that.
– Lingering pain. If the day could have passed more swiftly. But ever since early morning, each minute was pain . . . and pain had no relief.
– Lack of support. The thousands of people Jesus had helped— where where they? Even Christ's closest friends had fled. It seemed as though almost everybody in the world had sided with hatred, wanting love to die.

Yet, with all this crushing weight of sadness, Blessed Mary stood.

Where did she get her courage from? From faith, of course— God's gift enabling her to stand it. But there must have been other sources, too. Human ones. Mary had to be open to these currents of courage as well as to God's grace.

Perhaps one human source was the memory of her husband's patience. As she looked at Jesus on the cross and saw his helplessness, did she remember Joseph's helplessness as he was puzzling over what to do with her, before he had his dream? And did she remember how wonderful he was when he explained the dream to her? Did she remember his strength as they took flight into Egypt? And did she remember the calm ways he reassured her during the frantic search all over Jerusalem when Jesus was twelve years old?

Perhaps she did. And perhaps there were other friends who had given her comfort and stability in the past. She might have thought of them, too.

She also had friends right there, standing close to her. Perhaps Salome, wife of Chusa, held her hand. Maybe John supported her, holding her arm in his. They would have been a comfort. She was not alone.

That is the way most people are able to live through their periods of desolation. Mary would have been no different. God's grace, recollections of help by good friends in the past, appreciation of those who stay loyal during the actual time of sorrow—these are the sources of support. Without them, we falter . . . we can't stand it.

Let Mary be one of our staunch friends. She will guide us to Christ. She will open our memory to the courage we have known from others. And she will be present to us in the times of greatest need, providing us with an arm of support when we need it most.

Prayer

In your imagination,
take your place at the foot of the Cross. . . .
Stand right behind Mary. . . .

Imagine some of the thoughts
that might be going through her mind:
— thoughts about Joseph and his care;
— thoughts about her friends standing beside her;
— understanding about the mysterious ways of love
that came directly from God himself. . . .

Stay with these musings as long as possible. . . .

Then let John step out of the way.
He signals for you to take his place. . . .
You do. . . .
Take Mary's hand, in some way.
Remain there, next to her, looking at Jesus crucified. . . .

Feel good about being able to comfort her like this. . . .

Then pray to Mary, in your own words:
    ask the Mother of Sorrows to be a support to you
    when you have trials somewhat similar to hers. . . .

She will help you.
She knows how.
And she loves you, more than she ever did,
    because you took your place beside her. . . .
    You were with her.
    You helped her stand
        when it was so hard not to say,
        "I just can't stand it!"

29

Sorrow Without Blinders

Jesus, therefore, said to his mother, "Woman, behold your son."

John 19:26

Joseph [of Arimathea] took Jesus down from the cross and wrapped him in a linen cloth and laid him in a rock-hewn tomb . . . And the women . . . beheld the tomb and how his body was laid. And they went back . . .

Luke 23:50-56

Reflection

In the gospel of St. John, our Lord is almost tireless when he argues with his enemies. (See the long explanations of his "work," Chapters 6-8.) Also, he is quite articulate when he reasons with those who are confused: Nicodemus (John 3:1-21); the Samaritan woman (John 4:10-26); the apostles during the Last Supper (John 13:35-16:35).

But when Jesus spoke to those who understood him and thoroughly trusted him, he was amazingly sparing of words. Excluding the long prayer addressed to his Father (Chapter 17), dialogue between God and the Word of God is so terse it is bewildering (John 12:27-29):

"Now my soul is troubled.
What shall I say:
Father, save me from this hour?

But it was for this very reason
that I have come to this hour.
Father, glorify your name!"

[Then] a voice from heaven:
"I have glorified it,
and I will glorify it again."

We find the same economy of words whenever John records the dialogue between Jesus and his mother. Only twice does John mention the presence of Mary. On both occasions, the interchanges are so brief we must flesh out the words by study and prayer.

The first mention was at Cana, the inauguration of the ministry. To Mary's statement that "they have no wine," Jesus responded, "Woman . . . my hour has not yet come."

The second time, Mary did not speak at all. Once again, our Lord used few words. And once again, he was rather formal in the way he addressed his mother: "Woman, behold your son."

This manner of speaking is a far cry from saying "Mom" or "Mother." It was as if Jesus were establishing a diplomatic relationship. Mary was the woman—the universal earth mother bearing a brand new kind of offspring.

Then Jesus turned to the disciple who stood beside Mary. (Tradition has understood this man to be St. John himself.) He received his "adoption papers," too. Our Lord told him to regard Mary as his mother.

What a beautiful expression of thoughtfulness! Jesus was dying. His throat burned with such thirst that every utterance had to be very painful. Yet he made sure that his mother would be cared for. At that time, a widow without support was placed in a most perilous situation. No choice for her except beggary. Our Lord made sure this did not happen. John adopted her.

For Mary's part, however, this formal ceremony was much fuller. John received just one foster mother. Mary received everyone in the world. It was "Woman" who was addressed, the New Eve accepting all humans as her foster sons and daughters.

These words were the very last instruction Jesus made before he died. The Word of God made certain that his mother would be mother of us all. While the directive to "Behold your son" covers the widest range of humanity, it also had an immediate charge, a responsibility that would demand her attention that very night, as soon as she returned to the upper room.

Of course, Mary was sorrowful. Her sorrow was more dreadful than any person has ever been asked to bear . . . as she "beheld the tomb where the body was laid, and returned home."

Who has had more right to burst into rage, or moan with self-pity? People have quit on life who did not have nearly as much justification as Mary had. Many people, grieving from the pain of loss, put "blinders" on the sides of their eyes—blinders of mournfulness. When this happens, they cannot see anything but the causes of their own anguish. They restrict the world to such an extent that only their own bitter mood is attended to . . . and all the other people in their lives become unnoticed, unacknowledged.

Mary had no blinders. She was foster mother to many people already. She had neither the time nor the inclination to indulge in outrage or depression. There was work to do—the work of comforting assurance.

Oh, she suffered, yes. Feelings like sadness and grief and anger about injustice are not wrong. Mary felt them deeply. Often these feelings are the only appropriate reaction to an evil situation. Such feelings become wrong only when they control the rest of our lives.

Mary did not let this happen. Jesus told her to take care of the sons and daughters that she adopted. This she did. She returned to the upper room with the women who were with her. There she waited for the eleven apostles who would be returning soon—sheepishly ashamed of themselves—worried about what would happen next—looking at Mary (their mother, now) to see how she was coping with the crisis.

If Mary had given vent to her negative feelings, or chastised the disciples for their cowardice, or sulked in a corner, nursing the wounds of her personal sorrow—if Mary had done any of these things, everyone would have dispersed, quit on their discipleship, gone back home. There would have been nobody left to greet the risen Savior.

Mary knew her responsibility. She must "behold" her sons and daughters.

So she continued. She has continued ever since. She is the same source of maternal care for us, when we are grieving, as she was for the first disciples. She can teach us how to suffer as she did—to feel sorrow, deeply and honestly; and at the same time, not to be controlled by it . . . not to put blinders on.

Prayer

Remember the typical way
that you react negatively to a distressing situation:
- uncontrolled rage;
- repetitive scolding of people's wickedness or imperfections;
- getting paralyzed in your room;
- sulking in self-pity in front of others;
- any combination of these. . . .

Recall the most recent time
when you let your emotions get out of control this way. . . .

Now, in your imagination,
think of the places you are most familiar with:

- the place where you work (or go to school, etc.);
- your neighborhood;
- your own home.

Imagine that it is quitting time at work. . . .
Walk home, making the journey twice:

First time, put your "blinders" on.
Let yourself be aware only of your right to be upset. . . .
In such a mood, you will find that you take no notice of anyone;
you are not aware of anything but yourself:

- when fellow-workers call out to you, as you leave;
- when friends and neighbors
    try to greet you on your way;
- when family fails to get your attention
    once you are home. . . .

(These people have more of a right to your love
than you have a right to your bitterness.
But you don't see it that way. . . .)
Feel the lonely desolation of this experience
as long as you can stand it. . . .

Now return again, for a second journey.
Let Mary take the blinders away from you. . . .

> (She will not take away your sorrow.
> She can't do that,
> any more than she could take away her own.
> But she can take away
> the exclusive concentration on your sorrow. . . .)

Make the trip home, now, with a fresh alertness for others:
> – be attentive to co-workers as you leave;
> – be aware of friends and neighbors;
> – notice your family, sensitive to what is happening to
>   them. . . .

Let Mary point out the people
who especially need the hospitality of your care and affection. . . .
Let her help you with the right words—
> what to say
> and what not to say—
as she shows you, in many other ways,
how to be the source of loving care for others,
> even when you are down yourself. . . .

30

The Waiting Ordeal

And the women . . . beheld the tomb and how his body was laid.
And they went back home and prepared spices and ointments. And
on the Sabbath they rested, in accordance with the commandment.

Luke 23:55-56

Reflection

The history of the waiting period between Good Friday night and
Easter Sunday morning was just that—waiting.

Who knows how they passed the time. It was only two part-
days and one full Saturday. But those hours must have dragged,
dragged terribly. The women and the eleven did not know when, or
how, or even if they would ever get out of the upper room. The doors
were locked "out of fear." But how could a bolt on the door protect
them from a squad of soldiers? Every sudden street noise probably
pricked their ears. (Was it the Sanhedrin coming to arrest them?)

The apostles did not need outside disturbances to prick their
conscience. They were locked into their own fears, too. They had
proved to be cowards. They fell asleep when Jesus needed their
support. They ran away. Peter denied, by oath, that he even knew his
Lord. Whenever they glanced at Mary, their faces became more
ashen, their hearts even more ashamed.

Mary did not seem to hold a grudge against them. She was
helping them wait. But wait for what?

"Yes" (may have been the thoughts of the eleven), "Jesus did
say he would rise again. How did he say it, though? Does anyone

know for sure? He often spoke in figures of speech. Maybe he meant something else? Perhaps we heard him wrong? How is it possible that anyone can return from the dead?

"For he is dead. We know him to be buried, put away in a dark tomb. It's already been ten hours since it took place . . . no, ten hours and sixteen minutes. Oh, how slowly the time goes by! When is something—anything—going to happen?"

Probably, the locked-in disciples filled up part of the time with chantings and readings of Scripture. They would have turned the upper room into a makeshift synagogue, reading the required texts from the Law and the Prophets.

Perhaps, in this Sabbath liturgy, the gospel was proclaimed for the first time. After the Scripture readings, it might have been Simon Peter who interjected a remembrance of something Jesus had said. It is likely that our Lord's words were already coming true . . . when he said, "Simon, Satan has desired to have you, that he may sift you as wheat. But I have prayed for you, that your faith may not fail. And when you have turned again, [you will] strengthen your brethren" (Luke 22:31-32).

The way that he strengthened his brethren may have been to remind them about how often Jesus urged them to do just what they were doing—waiting.

It was only a few days before that Jesus had instructed them: "As he was near Jerusalem, he spoke a parable [of the talents] because they thought the kingdom of God was going to appear immediately" (Luke 19:11; Matthew 25:14ff).

The parable went on to speak of servants who were given certain sums of money before the king traveled abroad. He took a long time—longer than expected—before he returned to find how the servants managed in his absence. Our Lord insisted on this long time in order to inoculate his disciples against the virus of impatience, wanting God to do things immediately.

So many parables emphasized the same point. Five foolish virgins weren't prepared to "wait it out"; they were caught short when the bridegroom "took his time in arriving at the rendezvous point" (Matthew 25:1-13). Other servants, in other stories, decided "the Master delays his coming" and they began to get lazy and get drunk and browbeat their fellow servants (Matthew 24:45-51; Luke 12:41-46).

So many teachings insisted on the patient work of waiting. But it is so hard. Impatience is so easy. That was the quandry with the first disciples. After they celebrated their Liturgy of the Word—even after Peter's homily—what would they do with the rest of the thirty-six hours? Sleeping was probably out of the question. Small talk would have been insufferable. There could not have been any statements like "Cheer up" or "Look on the bright side!" There was no bright side.

Perhaps they paced the floor . . . they looked at each other's anxious faces . . . they found some comfort in the support of Mary's presence. Perhaps the women did some sewing; the men restrapped their sandals. We don't know. They probably couldn't remember if you asked them. All they would tell you were two things: 1) the time went very s . . . l . . . o . . . w . . . l . . . y, and 2) if Mary was not with them, they would have vanished like frightened animals, wasting the rest of their lives.

Mary's presence was a support for them, her patience was their model. But maybe she did more than give them good example. Maybe she spoke up, too . . . realizing that her sons and daughters needed more to think about. It was good for the disciples to remember that waiting is an important element of Christ's teaching. But this did not help them understand what they were waiting for. They realized that the kingdom would not appear immediately. But when would it come? And, when it came, what would it be like?

Mary would be the one to supply this answer. It might have been well after sundown when she decided words were necessary, to prevent total exasperation. Perhaps she gave them insights into how God might develop things, if only they waited well. Perhaps she gave them a share of the hope that she held on to.

Better than anyone, she could remind them of God's message to her, in Nazareth, when it all began. She was told to wait for Power from on high—"The Power of the Most High will overshadow you." So she did. Then she waited, long weeks, for Joseph to be told about it. Then she waited for the time to deliver Jesus into the world. It all turned out well. Life was the issue of her patience.

It was the same idea in the upper room. The disciples were doing what she had done, thirty-three years before. They were waiting for the Power of the Most High to work his love with them, passing through the locked doors of their doubts, issuing new life.

We too—same thing, same way—if only we will do the same, if only we ask Mary to be with us during the times when we hope for something to happen, but it hasn't happened yet.

Prayer

Remember one or two of your own personal experiences that
are somewhat like those excruciating hours
endured by the women and the apostles.
These would be your own version of being helpless to do anything
except to wait:
> – waiting for a loved one to change a lifestyle or a bad mood;
> – waiting for a letter that could make your life different;
> – waiting for God to relieve you of your tensions
>   or your sense of desolation;
> – or some other form of waiting. . . .

In your imagination,
put yourself in the upper room with Mary and the disciples. . . .
You notice what they are doing:
>   some occupying themselves with trivial things;
>   some crossing and uncrossing their legs
>   and looking worried. . . .
(You proceed to do the favorite things you do
    when you are upset and anxious and feeling helpless. . . .)

Take some consolation in the fact
that Mary is not scolding you
    for being so distressed.
She simply watches you with gentle eyes. . . .
She remains with you, a presence for you.

After a while, let her ask everyone to be quiet . . .
They all calm down.
You, too. . . .
All eyes look at her.
She looks at something no one else can see. . . .

She smiles.
Her face is radiant. . . .
Like a soft rain that gives healing to the parched earth,

she tells the story
of her "waiting times" at Nazareth:
- about how difficult it was for her;
- and how she did not know how the child would develop;
- and how she did not know when Joseph would
    understand. . . .
Now, as she looks back,
she knows how wonderfully it all worked out.
She tells you about it, in her own words. . . .

Finally, let her turn to you.
Let her give you reasons for renewed hope.
You have not come to the end of your life:
- the telephone may ring tomorrow;
- dryness in prayer may be transformed into consolations;
- thoughtless people may change (who knows when);
- the loved one may hit bottom,
    and then decide to be freed from the compulsion. . . .
        (Hitting bottom is not the end of life.
        Not even death is the end of life.
        Consider Easter—
            the best things happened
            after Christ had died. . . .)

Whatever way is the best way to reach you,
Mary will find it, if you give her time.
She will teach you how to cope with your distress
    so that you will be more comfortable with patience,
    and better able to wait . . . well. . . .

31

Wordless Prayer

On the first day of the week, at early dawn, (the women) came to the tomb . . . but they found the stone rolled back . . . On entering, they did not find the body of the Lord Jesus. And it came to pass, while they were wondering what to make of this, that [two angels] said, "Why do you seek the living one among the dead? He is not here. He is risen. . . ."

Luke 24:1-6

Reflection

The original Easter Sunday must have been a most confusing sequence of events. Even the evangelists, retelling the story years afterward, seem to be unsure about exactly how it happened. Did Jesus first appear to a group of women? (Matthew 28:9-10) Or was it to Mary Magdalen? (Mark 16:9; John 20:11-70) Or was it to the disciples walking in the country? (Luke 24:13; Mark 16:12) Or to Simon Peter? (Luke 24:34)

Whatever first happened, however the development of Christ's self-revelation occurred, we know this much: by nightfall, all the disciples (that is, the eleven apostles, a certain number of women, two people en route to Emmaus, and a large group of others) knew that Jesus had risen and had appeared to them.

One person was not included in any of these lists. Mary was probably a part of the various groupings. We know she was "with the disciples and the women" at Pentecost (Acts 1:14). There is no reason to suppose she was not present at Easter.

But we are not told. The gospels are written almost like a legal document—to verify that Jesus had all the necessary credentials to be the Messiah of the Jews and the savior of the people. His resurrection from the dead is "Exhibit A" among all his other credentials.

Therefore, the proclamation of Christ's resurrection had to be made by people who were qualified, so to speak. Legally, a mother cannot testify in her son's behalf. So Mary was not mentioned in the Easter passages. Her testimony would be considered "inadmissable" for proving to the authorities that Jesus is both Lord and God, the object of all reverence and the source of all our hope.

However, just because the evangelists did not choose to make a record of any meeting between mother and son, we cannot assume that such a meeting did not take place. Indeed, a very strong tradition from early times understands that Jesus made his presence known to Mary before he began his public revelations to the world at large.

A certain instinct tells us that this must have been so. There must have been a secret rendezvous somewhere in the city. Mary may have gone out early to draw fresh water from the well . . . something may have prompted her to walk farther, to an undisturbed part of town . . . and there Jesus appeared to her, in all his radiant beauty— telling her about his victory over death and what this victory meant for humankind.

We can say, "Maybe it happened something like this." But we do not know. It would not be wise to say any more about it. Better to follow the lead of all the gospels, and let silence shroud the mystery of Christ's first Easter message to his mother.

There are certain things that everyone must cherish in silence. It is likely that not even the apostles—not even the women who were so close to Mary—ever learned about that secret rendezvous. This was her own secret. It was so private, so cherished, that it would be spoiled if she tried to talk about it. Words, sometimes, are so inadequate. Better to be quiet than to convey a mystical experience that can be understood only by another mystic, one who is already familiar with the same wonder and intensity of God.

If this was the case, then we can please Mary best by honoring her need for privacy. Also, we can ask her to approve of the secrets that we keep within ourselves—the experiences of deepest prayer that are precious to us. They are so precious that we can know them only in wordless ways . . . and only the Lord is able to understand them.

Prayer

With your grateful memory to help you,
recall a time when you felt profound peace
linked to an intense moment of prayer.

(You may not have called it a mystical experience.
It may have seemed to be simply:
>   – the awareness of God, felt in a different way;
>   – an extraordinary expansive feeling about the beauty of
>   nature, or of your own worth;
>   – an almost overwhelming call to accomplish something
>   that would benefit others;
>   – some sense of being a vital part of Life—
>   Life larger, deeper, greater than ordinary life—
>   that came to you in the midst of people,
>   or in a place of solitude,
>   or in the dim consciousness of half-sleep. . . .)

Cherish this secret.
Try to recall a few more . . .
Present them to Jesus:
>   all that you can still remember;
>   and all that you have forgotten (but he remembers). . . .

Then, in your imagination,
meet Mary on a street in Jerusalem. . . .
She is returning to the upper room,
>   after she parted from her risen son. . . .

Offer to carry the jar of water for her. . . .
You walk in silence for a while . . .
Then you sit down on a porch step,
>   by an empty street. . . .
Just sit there in the stillness of early dawn,
>   saying nothing,
>   asking nothing,
>   not touching, not even glancing at one another;
>   just sitting. . . .

Let this simple gesture

convey your respect for Mary's need
    to be silent about her experience. . . .

And feel her respect for you.
By a kind of intuition,
    be assured of her approval of your silence . . .
This way you both know
    that there are some experiences
    you cannot put into words, or thoughts;
    not even to her. . . .

Stay with Mary, in this quiet place,
silently sharing the wonder of God's ways. . . .
Stay with it,
as long as it seems good to do so. . . .

PART FOUR

Mary
With Her New Family
After Easter

32

Self-Confidence

When it was late that same day [Easter], even though the doors where the disciples gathered had been locked for fear . . . Jesus came and stood in their midst and said to them, "Peace be to you." . . . The disciples therefore rejoiced at the sight of the Lord. He then said to them again, "Peace be to you. As the Father has sent me, I also send you."

John 20:19-22

Narration

(The time: five days after Easter. Simon Peter speaks:)

"I am finally getting used to the new situation. It wasn't easy, but at last I am living with my new-found joy a little easier.

"Don't be amazed by what I say. It is just as difficult to be at peace with an unexpected happiness as it is with unexpected despair.

It is just as overwhelming to have a sudden sense of great joy as it is to be jolted by a great sorrow. Both are crisis situations.

"Think a minute how it must have been with me. It was late in the afternoon, five days ago. We had heard rumors that Jesus was risen. Different women of our group had different versions about what happened at the tomb . . . and how the Lord appeared to them . . . and whether he told us to go to Galilee or stay here.

"We were all confused. Conflicting bits of news about the empty tomb could not relieve the intense sadness in our hearts. Good news had to be more than vague reports before it could change the shame we felt because we had run away from Jesus.

"We figured the women were making up those stories to try to cheer us up. We figured they meant well. But how could we believe them? Who had ever heard of someone rising from the dead? I must confess, we took more stock in our own feeling of shame and fear than we did in the message about the empty tomb.

"The doors were locked. We didn't want to see anybody. We were terribly afraid. Yes, part of it was fear that the authorities would come and put us in chains. But more than that, we were afraid of ourselves; we were so downhearted because of what we had done and had failed to do. The locks on the doors and windows were but a symbol of the way we were locked in our own selves.

"Nothing in my whole life could even come close to how dismal I felt—all of us. I remember that I resolved, right then, that I would never be arrogant any more. I would never again be high-handed toward anyone. I learned the lesson of my weakness . . . the hard way . . . and I would never have anything but gentle compassion for others who have their own weaknesses.

"These were my thoughts, when suddenly the whole world was changed around. Jesus came right through the doors, and he gave us peace. Amazing! He didn't scold us. He didn't tell us that he told us so. He didn't demand that we try to explain ourselves or promise not to let him down any more. He simply forgave us. He gave us peace.

"We came alive with joy. But the joy was too much to handle. Too much at once! So he said it again. Our Lord was so happy . . . he wanted so much for us to share his joy . . . he gave us peace a second time. He wanted us to calm down, you see, to stop feeling so dismal about ourselves.

"And then, most wonderful of all, he put confidence back into us. He said that we could do the job he had trained us to do for the last three years. He said it. We would not have presumed to do so. 'As the Father has sent me, I send you.' That's what he told us. Amazing.

"We had just proved that we couldn't be trusted. Yet he still trusted us. I was worse than the others. I had denied my Master, once with an oath. And yet Jesus forgave us. And then, as though we had never sinned, he told us that he had as much confidence in us as the Father had in him.

"It took a while before we could accept what he was saying. At first, we were simply overcome by it. Then we checked it out with each other. I still remember the muffled words: 'Did you hear what I heard!' 'Are your feelings the same as mine?' 'Do you think he meant this . . . and that . . . and the other thing . . . when he said, "As the Father has sent me, I send you"?' We kept checking out our thoughts, after the Lord had left.

"I was so glad Mary was with us. We all were. It wasn't so much what she said. She did have a marvelous way of putting into words what our hints and guesses were groping for. We appreciated that. But it was mostly her presence. Her smile. Her familiar gestures and her special way of assuring us that we were, indeed, forgiven.

"And it was the ordinary things she said . . . such as How much better we looked, now . . . How much color has come back into our cheeks . . . How we can use our gifts of leadership and love even better than we did before. Things like that.

"Mary solidified the joy and peace that Jesus gave us. Without her support, the risen Lord was still too much for us. Thanks to her, we were finally able to live with our new freedom, new courage, and new life.

"Mary can do the same for you, when you experience events similar to ours. Let her help you bring confidence back to your heart. She is very good at it."

Prayer

With your memory,
return to the most recent time
when you were in a dismal mood
and you felt guilty and ashamed
     because you had done something wrong. . . .

(You may have had thoughts of quitting on everything;
you at least had thoughts
    that the world would be better off without you. . . .)

It was a terrible time, locked into your misery.
Part of your mood was due to honest guilt:
    you were wrong.
Part of it was shame, born of false pride:
    "What will they think of me!"
    "How could I, of all people, have done such a thing!"

Then, somehow, you were freed from both sources of sorrow.
Perhaps it was the sacrament of reconciliation
such as Peter experienced it, Easter afternoon:
    Jesus, by means of his priesthood,
    forgave you your sins
    and freed you from both guilt and shame by his gift of
    peace. . . .

Perhaps it was a friend
who passed through the locked doors of your fears
and gave you reason to live again. . . .

Either way—or both ways—it has happened to you.
Thank God for making sure it happened;
and thank yourself for letting it take place.
Spend time with this. . . .
Be grateful for it. . . .

Then something else came, after you felt this peace.
It may have been some friends who noticed the change in you.
They observed that you were gentler than before,
    easier to be with,
    more mature, less irritable. . . .
Remember how good that made you feel
and how you gained more self-confidence
    thanks to their response. . . .

Now, in your imagination,
meet these friends again, in the same setting
    where they first remarked about the "new you". . . .

Let Mary join them.
Let her add to what they already said,
        giving you encouragement in her own way. . . .

And let her give you even more reason
to rejoice in Jesus' gift of peace—
        even more trust in his confidence
        as he sends you forth to do your work of love
        in the same way that his Father had sent him. . . .

33

Handling Anticipation

Now while they were talking about [all] these things, Jesus stood in their midst and said to them, "Peace be to you. It is I; do not be afraid." But they were startled and panic-stricken and thought they saw a spirit. And he said to them, "Why are you disturbed and why do doubts arise in your hearts?. . . ." But they still disbelieved and marveled for joy. So he said, "Have you anything here to eat?" And he said to them, " . . . I send forth upon you the promise of my Father. But wait here in the city until you are clothed with Power from on High.

Luke 24:36-38, 41, 49

Narration

(The time: soon after St. Luke's gospel was finsihed. Luke speaks:)
    "I wasn't present, you know, when Jesus said his last words to his disciples. It was some time afterward before I formally joined the community.
    "But I learned a great deal about it from the eyewitnesses of the event. I guess I always knew I would some day write an orderly account of the words and works of Jesus 'after following up all things carefully from the very first' (Luke 1:1).
    "Andrew was my best source. He remembered everything. He always knew where everybody was on each occasion. He could recall, in detail, how one thing developed from another.
    "The others were not as clear. Matter of fact, they were confusing at times—especially when they reminisced about Easter and its aftermath. Peter and John would say one thing; Thomas, another; Matthew had a different sense of it; the women would give their

version. Sometimes they were all talking at once! The garbled testimonies were almost humorous at times. Certainly hectic.

"I tried to capture this mood in my gospel. Even though the disciples had already experienced the risen Lord, they were still afflicted. They were startled and panic-stricken when Jesus appeared to them again. They admitted having doubts in their hearts: 'What would life be, what will it mean, now that life has been so dramatically changed by Christ?'

"You see, they were sure that death was the end of everything. After death, goodbye! Now they had to rethink death; and rethink what it will be like to live, now that death is not a finality . . . now that it became an ushering-in of new life, greater than before.

"Seeing Jesus alive after death overwhelmed them. They thought he was a spirit, even though their eyes and ears and the touch of his hands and side told them otherwise. They blocked off their joyful hearts to such an extent that their consciousness judged Jesus to be an apparition.

"That's when the Lord asked them for a piece of fish. He took the food, chewed it, swallowed it. He enjoyed a leftover from an earlier meal! That did it. That calmed them down. No spirit eats a fish sandwich. Jesus was the same as he was before he died . . . even though he was different, too.

"I wanted to capture all this in my written account. The Easter reports were like a fast-moving river butting against the onrushing waves of the sea—there were strong certainties clashing against each other, causing a great spray of conflicting emotions. Still the truth was evident, and it was accepted . . . even though it was registered in befuddled ways.

"For all these reasons, I decided to be not so orderly when I wrote my account of the Easter appearances. I had to be honest to my sources.

"Yet on one point they were quite decisive and unanimous. There was no question about what the Lord's last words were, and what it meant. They were told to wait. In God's good time, in the way that he saw fit, they would receive 'Power from on high.'

"This time, the waiting was not a distressing experience. All the disciples agree on this, too. It was not at all like the terrible ordeal of waiting they endured a few days before. Indeed, they went back to the city and praised God with great joy as they waited for the sending of the Holy Spirit.

"Mary was the key to their change of heart. She reminded them of what she had said earlier. They heard her then; but they did not fully comprehend because they were too locked in to their own fears, too crushed by their own guilt. Now, things were different. Jesus had opened their ears as well as their hearts, when he gave them peace and confidence.

"Mary helped them understand this mystery of receiving Power from on High. I was so moved by the beautiful way the apostles told me about Mary's wisdom. She assured them that they could expect their own version of her annunciation.

"It was then that I decided to highlight the theme of God's Power. That is why I began my gospel with one annunciation and ended it with the other. With Mary, the message was 'Wait . . . and the Power of the Most High will overshadow you' (Luke 1:35). With the disciples, the message was 'Wait until you are clothed with Power from on high' (Luke 24:49).

"It is the same reality, the same Spirit of God, the same need to wait. Just a different way of receiving the Power.

"So it is with you, with every Christian. Mary will be with you as you prepare for new directions to your life. She will help you change your period of expectancy—instead of being filled with doubts about yourself, befuddled with conflicting moods, or panic-stricken over the loss of certainties . . . Mary will prepare you with hopefulness and train you to wait for Power from on high."

Prayer

In your memory,
recall some good "waiting times" in your life:
  – waiting to have a baby;
  – waiting for graduation
        and the commencement of life in a larger school.
  – waiting to receive your driver's license
        and have the power to handle your own car;
  – waiting to be married
        or to be received into a religious community;
  – waiting for word about a new job, a new assignment;
  – whatever. . . .

(Remember that you had doubts, too;
as well as hopeful expectations. . . .

There was confusion in your heart
    caused by some regret about what would be lost.
There was also anxiety
    about how good the gain might turn out to be. . . .
Remember these things.
Experience the clash of emotions once again. . . .)

Now think of some new changes of life
that are still in your future:
        – a new opportunity that might open up;
        – a different home or place of employment;
        – another child,
            or a quieter life now that the children are grown up;
        – retirement, and the new power of wisdom you will have,
            when the routine of work won't drain you;
        – a different calling to serve the church or the world;
        – whatever. . . .

In your imagination,
sit in a favorite chair, in a favorite room. . . .
Outside this room is a larger room
where Christ's first disciples are all assembled . . .
(They continue to buzz with excitement,
even though Jesus left them a few hours before. . . .)

You remain in your own room,
thinking about the possible changes in your life. . . .
Mary knocks on the door.
Welcome her, in whatever way seems right. . . .
Tell her about your thoughts—
    your hopes,
    and your doubts, too. . . .

Let her assure you about the new Power
soon to be given you:
    the Power she was given when she began God's plan of love;
    the Power promised to all disciples of her son. . . .

Stay with this as long as it is good . . .
Then go with her to the large room
    and listen to their stories. . . .
    and share their joy. . . .

34

Letting Go Gracefully

They returned to Jerusalem . . . to the upper room where they were
staying. [The apostles] with one mind continued steadfast in prayer
with the women and Mary, the mother of Jesus. And when the day of
Pentecost drew to a close . . . they were filled with the Holy Spirit
and [all] began to speak in foreign tongues, as the Holy Spirit
prompted them to speak . . . about the wonderful works of God . . .
Then Peter . . . lifted up his voice and spoke out to them, "Men of
Judea and all you who dwell in Jerusalem, let this be known
to you and give ear to my words...."

Acts 1:14-2:14

Narration

(The time: many years after Pentecost. Andrew speaks:)

"I remember Pentecost as if it were yesterday. Not all the
positive aspects of Pentecost: the sureness of Christ's presence and the
gifts of his Spirit, and the wonderful things we did and said. These are
not 'as if yesterday'; they are still today.

"No, I'm talking about the one bad aspect about the event. It
wasn't bad, actually. Somebody had to get the crowd to quiet down.
There had to be one voice to speak for all of us, to interpret what went
on that day. My brother was chosen to assume this kind of leadership
role. He did it. It was good that he did.

"The only thing 'bad' about it was my initial feeling—my 'gut
reaction,' as you would say. I wasn't jealous, not really. The Holy
Spirit was with me too strongly to be that small-minded. But I admit I

was tempted to be jealous. The first 'click' of my emotions, was, 'Oh boy! There he goes again! My brother is taking over the whole show! Just when we're all enjoying ourselves, he's telling us to take a back seat so he can speak up!'

"As you know, Pentecost was not the first time such a thing happened. There were a lot of yesterdays to back up that yesterday. It seems I was always running second to my brother. After all, I was the one who discovered Jesus. I told Simon, then we went together to be his disciples (John 1:35-42). We were partners in the fishing business. (I'm not telling which is the older; that's our secret.)

"It wasn't long before my brother became the favorite. Peter, James and John went to the house of Jairus (Mark 5:21-43). I was left behind to manage things in the Lord's absence. Then the same three witnessed the transfiguration on Mount Tabor. And where was I? As usual—down in the valley, supervising things . . . minding the store, so to speak, while the other three were having a wonderful time (Mark 9:1-6).

"This happened many times. Oh, I know I had my special gifts. Jesus relied on me a great deal. I was the vice-master, in a way, during the three-year training period of our discipleship.

"I was a good observer. I notice things. Remember, I was the one who saw the boy with those barley loaves and fish (John 6:8-10). I was the negotiator for people who wanted an interview with the Master (John 12:22). These were my gifts. But it was hard, sometimes. My brother was in on the action and I was left behind to make sure things didn't get disorganized.

"Oh, there were moments of exhilaration. Don't get me wrong. I was one of the disciples sent out to perform miracles and preach in Christ's name. I witnessed the Lord's joy when we returned to tell him all about it (Luke 10:17). But I didn't have as many occasions for this joy as the others did. Besides, I was the best cook in the group. So I got stuck with this chore more than the others. But that's another story.

"I wanted to give you this background so you would understand how good it felt for me to express myself so freely when Pentecost gave me the power to praise the wonderful works of God.

"It was so exciting to hear the words come out of my mouth— just the right words—and know I was understood by the people of Parthia, in their own language! All of us—the eleven, the women, and Mary too—all of us speaking to one particular language group as the Spirit directed.

"I could have gone on forever! Then my brother told us to quiet down. It took some discipline for me to do so. I wanted to tell him to quiet down . . . to let me speak up for a change. The Spirit was supplying me with words that were just as good as his. And anyway, although I did run away from Jesus on Good Friday, at least I didn't deny that I knew him. Simon was a worse sinner than I. So he should be the least qualified to be our spokesman.

"These were temptations going through my mind and the quickened pulse of my heart. Then I looked at Mary. She quieted down, too. I noticed her earlier. She was having as good a time as I was. And she had been silenced a lot longer than I. It was about thirty-three years since she publicly praised God for the wonderful things that were done through her. Since she sang her Magnificat to Saint Elizabeth, hers was a quiet life . . . quieter than mine.

"And she had more reason than I to tell my brother to back down and let her do the talking. After all, she didn't sin in any way. She was one of the few people who were faithful, even on Good Friday.

"Yet she complied with Simon's call to silence. She didn't even seem to mind. Her face was composed. She was serene. She simply stopped what she was doing and patiently listened to what my brother would say.

"That helped me. I took my cue from her. I did not give in to jealousy. I restrained myself from starting a family quarrel. I had my job. Peter had his. Jesus directed him to 'feed my sheep.' He did. It all went well.

"Now we have gone our separate ways. I still have a leadership role, according to the gifts God gave me. But I'll never forget that beautiful experience on Pentecost. And I'll never forget to be grateful to Mary, for helping me calm down so that I could graciously defer to someone else."

Prayer

Think of the times when,
to some extent,
you had to do what Andrew had to do.

This could be noted under a number of headings:
- athletes who get benched by better athletes;
- parents who find that their children, in certain ways,
    prove to be more capable than they are;
- teachers, administrators, executives, nurses, union leaders . . .
    who are sidelined in favor of younger talent;
- put in other instances, personal to you. . . .

In your memory,
recall the resentment you felt when you were pushed aside
    so that someone else could lead
    or handle the situation. . . .
Reawaken the first shock you felt
and the words you said (or wanted to say):
- how you still have very important things to say;
- how you aren't that old, and your talents
    should not be treated so lightly;
- how your ideas are just as good as somebody else's;
- things like that (the typical ways that you rehearse your
    grievance about being upstaged. . . .)

Then stop the clamor of these thoughts.
In your imagination
go to a high school baseball field. . . .
It is deserted.
There is only one small set of bleachers.
Imagine the "game of life" going on without you,
    moved by a leadership that is no longer yours. . . .

Mary walks by,
notices you,
comes up to sit beside you. . . .
Tell her, in your own words, about your distress. . . .

Let her listen,
asking questions, when appropriate. . . .

Then let her tell you
about how it was with her, at Pentecost. . . .
And let her remind you that this must be the case

with everyone—
    we grow older;
    we slow down;
    others are given authority that we once had;
    our work is somewhere else. . . .

Let her help you with serenity
(the kind that she and Andrew had)
    so that you may gently let go of controls
    when it is time to do so. . . .

35

Slowing Down the Pace

Now in those days, as the number of the disciples was increasing, there arose a murmuring among [one group] against [another group] that their widows were being neglected in the daily ministrations. So the Apostles called together the multitude of the disciples and said, "It is not desirable that we should forsake the word of God and serve at tables. Therefore, select from among you seven men of good reputation, full of the spirit and wisdom, that we may put them in charge of this work. But we will devote ourselves to prayer and to the ministry of the word." And the plan met with the approval of the whole multitude, and they chose Stephen . . . and Philip . . . and [five more.]

Acts 6:1-5

Narration

(The time: a few months after the above took place. Deacon Philip speaks:)

"It seems that the decision of Simon Peter and the other apostles to share some of their administrative burdens has been working out well. If I do say so myself, we are doing a better job than they did.

"It wasn't their function, actually. It wasn't their talents. They were on the verge of what you would call 'burnout.' There was no time left to take care of their primary responsibilities—preaching, studying the Scriptures, discovering connections between the life of Jesus and the writings of the Law and the Prophets . . . and understanding what all this means to us, now that our community is growing.

"These tasks demanded their full time. But they were stuck with another full-time job—trying to distribute the food and clothing (farm land, also) that we held in common—fair share to everybody, without showing favoritism.

"But favoritism did come up. Only natural, I guess. The apostles couldn't resist giving the best food and clothing to the families of their friends. These people had served in the cause of Christ much longer than the strangers who came from Greek-speaking towns. Without thinking, friends got the better deals in the distribution.

"So a lot of bitterness erupted. Squabbling. You know how such a thing can happen. Jealousies and hurt feelings were so prevalent around the supply depot, you could get poisoned by just breathing the air.

"The eleven tried to do what was fair. Still, nobody seemed to be satisfied. We could see their long faces, hear their short tempers. They were getting bags under their eyes.

"We went to Mary, asking if she was concerned about it. Maybe she could think of something. Yes, she was concerned. She told us about another time, during her son's ministry, when her family came to her with the same complaint. 'Your son is working too hard,' they said. 'He should slow down and come home.'

"But that was a different case, Mary told us. Jesus was spending himself on things that were vital to his ministry. The apostles were wearing themselves thin over things that were secondary. Perhaps there was another way to meet these administrative demands . . . and free the leaders for what is more important.

"Mary made a few suggestions. We added some ideas of our own. And we prayed together and promised to pray on it some more. Then, somehow (we're not exactly sure, but Stephen and I did see Mary talking privately with Peter and James) somehow it was decided that deacons should be established.

"That's right. We would be called deacons. We would preach and assist at the Eucharist. But our primary task was to distribute to our people all the goods we had in common.

"As I said, it worked out well. We were freer to do our job. The apostles became freer to do theirs.

"I'm telling you all this because it may help you in the practical economics of your division of labor. There are some tough decisions you may have to make in the rearranging of your time.

"It may be comforting to know that good people suffered on the brink of 'burnout' centuries before you were born (centuries before the word burnout was born). We had to adjust, to make changes because of added demands put upon our lives. The apostles had to share responsibilities. They had to admit they couldn't do everything themselves. Mary was the one who put them at peace about it.

"She can do the same for you. You're not much different. You probably have too many things to do, and not enough time to do them. You probably feel you have to meet an overload of deadlines, also. You probably have to produce more than you can handle. Doubtless, there are 'murmurers' in your life, too—demanding so much of your time, so much of your presence, that you cannot find either the place or the peace to pray to God or think about the most important aspects of your life.

"Let Mary help you as she helped us. Let her pray for you. She will advise you, privately, about how you can possibly reschedule things, or farm out some responsibilities, or somehow arrange your blocks of time so that you can be more open to God, and to the really important parts about yourself."

Prayer

In your imagination,
go to a room
that contains all the clutter of your "busy-ness":
  – telephones clanging;
  – TV programs pulling you into their problems;
  – adults and children barging in, full of expectations
      that you listen to their woes or give them comfort;
  – long lists of things you have to do;
  – letters to write, obligations to meet;
  – vaguely felt guilt feelings because you didn't do
      this or that for one person or another;
  – such things. . . .
Get a headache from all the pressure of it. . . .

Then relax. . . .
Think of one or two friends who really care about you
     (who are not demanding).
Let them quietly come into your room.
You see their concern for you. . . .
They silence the phone, turn off the TV,
     take away all those symbols of your hectic pace. . . .
Breathe slowly and easily.
You are free, for a while, of expectations. . . .

Let Mary join you there.
Let her speak privately
as she did to the apostles:
     – suggesting different ways of regulating your time;
     – reminding you about the necessity of prayer,
          and about other necessities
          that you have neglected to give quality time for. . . .

Do not argue with Mary.
Do not answer back with any statement that begins "Yes, but . . ."
Do not say anything at all.
Just listen
     as though you were hearing these suggestions
     for the first time. . . .

Probably Mary's suggestions will not be new.
You've heard them before,
But you never really listened.
     (You brought up so many objections to the idea;
     you have attempted change so reluctantly;
     nothing happened.)
Now hear the suggestions as Mary presents them to you.
Hear them with hope. . . .

Finally, promise Mary, in your own words,
that you will pray more about these suggestions. . . .
Thank her. . . .
Perhaps you could ask her to return in a few days
     to talk about it again. . . .

And say goodbye, in whatever way seems right. . . .

36

Open to Fresh Ideas

After a long debate, Peter got up and said, "God gave the Holy Spirit to the Gentiles, just as he did to us. . . ." [When Peter and others] had finished speaking, James made this answer, saying, "Brethren, listen to me. Simon has told how God first visited the Gentiles to take from among them a people to bear his name . . . Therefore, my judgment is not to disquiet those . . . who are turning to the Lord."

Acts 15:7-11; 13-19

Narration

(The time: a few months after the first council in Jerusalem. The wife of James speaks:)

"Things are going more smoothly, now. My husband hasn't clenched his fists in weeks. He's easier to get along with. Less tense. Less irritable. At last, he agreed to take the world off his shoulders.

"But it wasn't easy for him. You know how inflexible some people are. My husband James is a very good man. So dedicated. So enthusiastic for the God movement Jesus began. But enthusiasts can be difficult to live with, sometimes. They get carried away with their own style of life; and nobody can persuade them that other ways of life can be good, even better. They cannot readily adapt to new challenges, or to change their ways . . . even though it is obvious to other people that they ought to change.

"James did not think he was inflexible. (Such people never do!) Simon Peter, Paul, Barnabas, and practically all the others thought so. But James was convinced he was sticking to principles. He insisted that the new converts must be saddled with all the picky-picky prescriptions of the Mosaic Law before they could be accepted as Christians.

"Then God himself tried to move him. He arranged a whole series of marvelous events, just a few weeks before the convocation (Acts 10:1-29; 34-48). Simon Peter told us all about his dream, and then what happened to the pagan family of Cornelius. God was telling him—telling us all—that 'we should not call any person common or unclean.'

"James thought that series of miracles was just an exception to the rule. The rule prevailed! He sided with the minority who were inflexible about their opinions. No change! The Jewish bigotry against the rest of the world must stay as bad as their bigotry against us. So things would continue as they were. Gentile converts must knuckle under to laws they could not follow because, as my husband argued, 'It must be so!'

"I worried about James during that long heated debate. His brows were furrowed. Fists were clenched. He shouted more than he had to.

"Fortunately, further argument was postponed. It was almost time for supper. Somebody suggested that we all go off and pray by ourselves. Most took a walk. I saw my husband go to the quiet room set apart for meditation. Mary followed him. (I watched from the door.)

"She said nothing to him. She was silent for a while. Then she prayed out loud, loud enough for James to hear the words.

"Then—Oh, it was so beautiful the way she did it—then she took up his right hand. (It was still clenched.) She gently opened up the fingers. One by one, they settled to a relaxed position. She was warming his hand with her two hands. Then they prayed together. (I couldn't hear.)

"After supper, James was a changed man. He relented his unbending approach. He understood the graciousness of God by being with the graciousness of Mary. Then he became gracious. (I never loved him more than I did that day.) He made the proposal about what Gentile converts must do so that they would not upset Jewish converts. The rules were very easy. All agreed it was a good proposal. It did not disquiet anyone.

"James saved the day. I like to believe that he saved the church at that most crucial meeting. But he would not have done it if it weren't for Mary. It was her love for the new converts—her sons and daughters, as she always called them—that provided the bending to James's unbending ways. It was that little 'message of love' given to his clenched fist that made the difference.

"She can make a difference for you, too. She has a way about her . . . it is her gentleness and love . . . that can ease the tensions caused by bitterness or bigotry or any other determination to remain inflexible.

"Mary can help you. She is the best there is."

Prayer

Think of one or two precious opinions of yours—
those fixations you are inflexible about. . . .

(You would not call yourself inflexible.
You are convinced your stand is based on solid facts,
well thought out,
righteously adhered to . . .
But friends think you are inflexible;
and good people of sound mind may think so, too . . .
Nevertheless, you stick to your opinions. . . .)

Go to a room where there are various symbols—and maybe
slogans—representing your fixed opinions . . .

Now clench your fist.
Let this be the sign
of how tenaciously you will defend your ideas
against all criticism. . . .

Then let Mary come into your room. . . .
Let her be with you as she was with James. . . .
She prays silently, beside you. . . .
Then she prays out loud,
loud enough so that you can hear what she is saying. . . .

Be open to the possibility
that she is asking God to soften your self-righteousness

and asking you to look at situations
    from a kinder, more humane point of view. . . .

Then let her take your hand (still doubled up in a fist)
and gently smoothe it out. . . .
holding your hand in hers, to give it warmth. . . .

Stay with this sense of Mary's presence. . . .
But do not be concerned that you get no practical advice.
    (This will come after your prayer—
    after Mary has changed your mood,
    after she had transformed your hand and heart
    into a gesture of graciousness. . . .)

37

Preparing for Perfect Happiness

When [the disciples saw Peter] they were amazed. But he motioned to them with his hand to be quiet and he related how the Lord had brought him out of prison. And he said, "Tell this to James and to the brethren." And he departed and went to another place.

The last words of St. Peter
Acts 12:16-17

Narration

(The time: many years after the council in Jerusalem. The place: unknown. John speaks:)

"Sorry about being so secretive, but the authorities are still searching for us. I must be circumspect.

"Blessed Mary, as you know, has been in my charge. Ever since Good Friday. We left Jerusalem soon after the council in 49. We did it the same way Simon Peter did—a motion with the hand for quiet; then the mention that we were departing 'for another place.' What the disciples don't know won't hurt them.

"We embraced, said our goodbyes, gave final words of encouragement, and here we came. It has been a very good life. The community is growing. We do exchange information with the other churches. We learn the news this way. I personally have learned much from the letters of Paul and the records written by Mark, Matthew, and Luke.

"The Holy Spirit (Mary helping me) has suggested that I write down a record of Jesus, too—different from the others, putting a fresh slant on the significance of what our Lord said and did. This will balance the picture, make it more complete.

"I have learned a great deal from Mary. She taught me to pray in a deeper, calmer way. She told me many things about the quiet life in Nazareth. She also counseled me about what was not essential, not necessary. I wanted to write books and books about what happened to Jesus, and what it means to us. I wanted to fill a whole library with what I knew. She applied the brakes to my enthusiasm. She kept telling me to pray about it, to discipline myself for the essentials. I did. I'm almost finished now.

"Mary has died. A few years ago. I won't go into the particulars. Mary said I shouldn't. I can tell you this much: It was beautiful. She was beautiful. I have seen many people die peacefully; never did I see such a face of peace and joy as Mary's was. I have expelled demons from many people, and have seen how different they looked—how full of life and high spirits—once the devil left them. But Mary, at the moment of her death, showed me how full life can be when it is freed from the weight of sin and the influence of the devil.

"Her death was different from any other. There was a bright light all around her and a sense of perfect happiness that she was already experiencing. I saw it in her face.

"According to instructions, I buried her in a stone tomb. (One just like the tomb in which Jesus was laid.) Noboby came with me. I carried her and placed her down on a cot, rolled a stone over the entrance and went away. Nobody knows where it is. A few shepherds have guessed, but they steer clear of the place. The details will die with me.

"Anyhow, it doesn't matter. I know she has been taken away from there, her body as well as her spirit. Just as God did not allow his son to remain long in his tomb, but raised him up to new life . . . so did God do the same for his mother.

"It had to be. I know it by intuition. Don't have facts. Don't need them. Mary has told me, so often, about the beautiful events surrounding the birth of Jesus. Luke and Matthew have already written about these things. I have been helped by them, but even more by Mary. The Word of God was God. For all eternity, the Son of God already is.

"And then God decided to step into our time, into our world. He asked for Mary's help. She agreed. She conceived the Word of God, so that God could be a human, just as we are.

"It was because of what she had done in the past that she knew what God would do for her, in the near future. As she was dying, she told me about her certainty. She smiled when she told me: 'It will be the first time a son ever gave birth to his mother.'

"That's the way she expressed it. True enough. Because Mary did such a good job in bringing God into our world, Jesus would soon bring Mary into his world—heaven.

"And so it happened.

"And now I have her hope to hang on to, when I prepare to die. I can look forward to the same thing. Oh, I don't presume that I am as thoroughly good as Mary. I've had my displays of temper. (Jesus did not call my brother and me 'Sons of Thunder' for nothing!) I used to be vain, wanting places of honor for James and myself. (Only later did I realize that closeness to the Lord meant being a familiar of his passion.) Also, I fell asleep on Jesus that night in Gethsemane. I ran away.

"Even so, for the most part I did the same thing Mary did. I heard the word of God and kept it. I let it 'take flesh' in me. And I have brought forth the Word, conditioned by my gifts and personality, so that others could benefit by my life in Christ. Peter and Paul brought forth the Word, made of their flesh. Martha and Mary of Bethany did so their way. Matthew, Mark, and Luke manifested their 'incarnation of God' according to their gifts and writing style. We all are 'mothers of God' in this sense—not in the same way that Mary was, but it is the same reality.

"And we all have the same 'turnabout' to hope for. I know it to be so. It is my faith. Mary coached me in the mystery of how wonderful life will be after I die. Jesus will bring me forth into his world, because I have done a reasonably good job of bringing him forth into mine.

"Mary will help you, too. Same way. With the same hope. Then you will have no more reason to fear death than I. You can expect the same 'birthing' by our Lord by which Mary has been blessed—forever."

Prayer

In your imagination,
go to your favorite bed.
Lie down, head propped against pillows. . . .

Recall some of the good things you have done with your life:
    (Do not infect these thoughts with any negative side issues.
    Do not say: "Yes, but I could have done better!"
    or: "Yes, but why didn't they appreciate me!"
Simply reflect that you did good things
    because good was good to do.)

Acknowledge before God
that these were some of the ways
    by which you "brought forth the Word of God
        made of your flesh"
    as opportunity offered
    and as your unique gifts made possible. . . .
Enjoy these thoughts as long as you can,
without discomfort. . . .

Now think of the time when you are about to die,
whenever that might be. . . .
You are propped up in a reclining chair,
    pillows supporting you comfortably. . . .
Invite some cherished friends to be with you. . . .
    (It doesn't matter whether they are dead or far way.
    Meditation deals with the possibilities of prayer;
    your own memory will make them as real, and as close,
        as God wants them to be. . . .
    Let the Holy Spirit suggest the ones who should be there.
    Do not try to think of them—just let them come to mind. . . .)

Watch them as they take up all your good deeds,
one by one,
and make a warm patch quilt of them, to cover you. . . .

Let Mary join your friends. . . .
Let her tell you of the joy she had,
the day she died. . . .
(It may be she will simply present you with a sense of it,
rather than describe it.

Somehow, she will let you understand. . . .)

Ask her to give you some of her confidence. . . .
Ask her to help you look forward to life after death
    with the same trust that was hers. . . .

And finally, ask her for some practical advice:
about how you can do more good in this life—
    more "bringing forth God's love, made of your flesh"—
so that you will have an even better quilt to cover you. . . .
so that you may have even more confidence in Christ,
    more peace,
    as you prepare for perfect happiness. . . .